The ORCA SCIENTISTS

by Kim Perez Valice
With photographs by Andy Comins and the Center for Whale Research

Houghton Mifflin Harcourt

Boston   New York

For Jim and the boys —KPV

The illustrations in this book were done digitally.
The text type was set in Interstate.
The display type was set in Brandon Grotesque and Umbra Std.
Photo credits can be found on page 77.

Library of Congress Cataloging-in-Publication Data is on file.

ISBN 978-0-544-89826-4

Manufactured in Malaysia
TWP 10 9 8 7 6 5 4 3 2 1
4500698468

CONTENTS

Prologue.. 4

Beyond Black and White 9

Best Catch of the Day 22

Pump Up the Volume 35

It Makes Perfect Scents... 49

Mission Mobley Soars... 56

What the Future Holds 69

How to Get Involved and Stay Informed 72

Glossary 73

Selected Bibliography and Sources 74

Acknowledgments & Author's Note 76

Photo Credits 77

Index 78

PROLOGUE

In the early 1970s, the marine mammal biologist Dr. Mike Bigg began to count every orca he saw. Orcas were being captured for marine parks, and the Canadian Department of Fisheries and Oceans in Nanaimo, British Columbia, was concerned that there weren't enough whales to support the captures. Mike turned to local fishermen, lighthouse keepers, fishery patrol boats, tugboat captains, and others who lived and worked along the coast of British Columbia, where the whales were often spotted. He asked them to take count during the months of July and August from 1971 to 1973. There were fifteen thousand questionnaires distributed to these individuals, who took note of the population. Over the three years, Mike tallied data that showed an estimated 200 to 350 whales living in the waters off British Columbia. This number seemed much lower than most people expected.

In addition to counting, Mike began photographing the orcas' fins. At the time, photo identification was an unexplored method for scientists. However, it worked perfectly for Mike. The physical characteristics of what a specific whale's fin looked like soon became easily identifiable. Each orca could be identified by its dorsal fin and unique saddle patch. Mike found the saddle patches to be like fingerprints

In the 1960s, Dr. Mike Bigg pioneered this new method of photo identification that is now a tried-and-true practice in the field of science.

in humans—every patch unique to an individual whale. Mike could follow each whale, then determine where they traveled. With every encounter, Mike and his team became accustomed to finding the whales swimming together in groups, or pods, containing ten to twenty-five or more whales.

On Canada's North Vancouver Island, where Mike began his study, he named the first group of travelers the A pod. Each individual in the A pod received a number, starting with 1. The next group he found swimming together, he named the B pod; then came the C pod, D pod, and so on. The alphabet pods continued until Mike reached the letter I. The I pod swam close to the southern tip of Vancouver.

On occasion Mike noticed smaller groups of two to five whales traveling together. Finding these small groups in the same spot seemed less predictable: they never swam in larger pods. They also traveled to different areas and ate different prey. Could it be that these whales were the social outcasts? Possibly. Mike termed them *transients*. The whales that traveled in larger groups were called *residents*. Because the orca whale pods from letters A to I ate only fish and typically inhabited the waters in northern Vancouver, he named them Northern Residents.

As Mike worked his way toward South Vancouver and into United States waters, the whale biologist Ken Balcomb joined in the search. A Washington resident, Ken knew of Mike's study, and it was near Ken's area where the next pods

When Ken started studying the whales, people responded with, "Why? What good are they?" Ken says, "My best response was to point out that as top marine predators, whales are indicators of the health of the environment in which they live—the ocean—and that is also an environment upon which humans depend."

of fish-eating whales swam. Mike and Ken found three pods, which they named J, K, and L. These whales soon became known as the Southern Residents. Ken still uses Mike's tried-and-true database as the primary way to track the births, deaths, and pod formation of the orca whales he encounters.

Even today the Southern Resident orca whales reside in U.S. waters south of Canada, and the Northern Residents live in Canadian waters, north of the Salish Sea. The Salish Sea includes the southwestern portion of British Columbia and the northwest portion of Washington State. It's common for the pods to disperse as they head for different areas to find food. While the Js stick around Washington's San Juan Island area all year, the Ks and Ls head to Oregon and as far south as Monterey Bay, California, for the winter months.

Mike Bigg passed away in 1990, but Ken continued to identify both resident and transient orcas in these waters. Today he concentrates on identification of both the resident and transient orca whale population in Washington and southern Canada. He is considered an expert in the field, and his research has laid the foundation for the identification of various orca species that exist throughout the world.

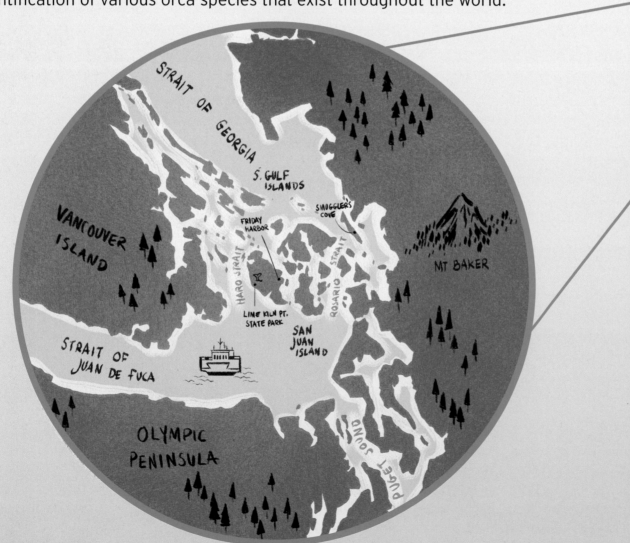

STRAIT OF GEORGIA

S. GULF ISLANDS

SMUGGLERS COVE

VANCOUVER ISLAND

FRIDAY HARBOR

HARO STRAIT

LINE KILN PT. STATE PARK

SAN JUAN ISLAND

ROSARIO STRAIT

MT BAKER

STRAIT OF JUAN DE FUCA

OLYMPIC PENINSULA

PUGET SOUND

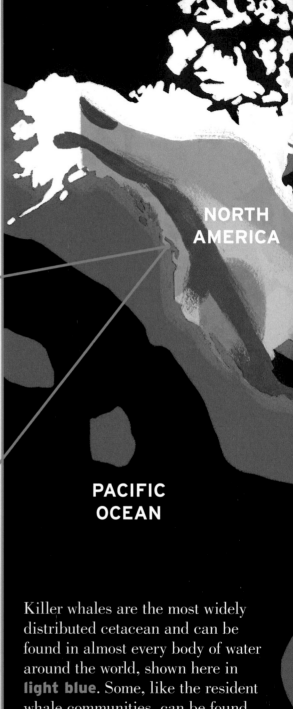

NORTH AMERICA

PACIFIC OCEAN

Killer whales are the most widely distributed cetacean and can be found in almost every body of water around the world, shown here in **light blue**. Some, like the resident whale communities, can be found in large numbers along coastlines where there's an abundance of prey.

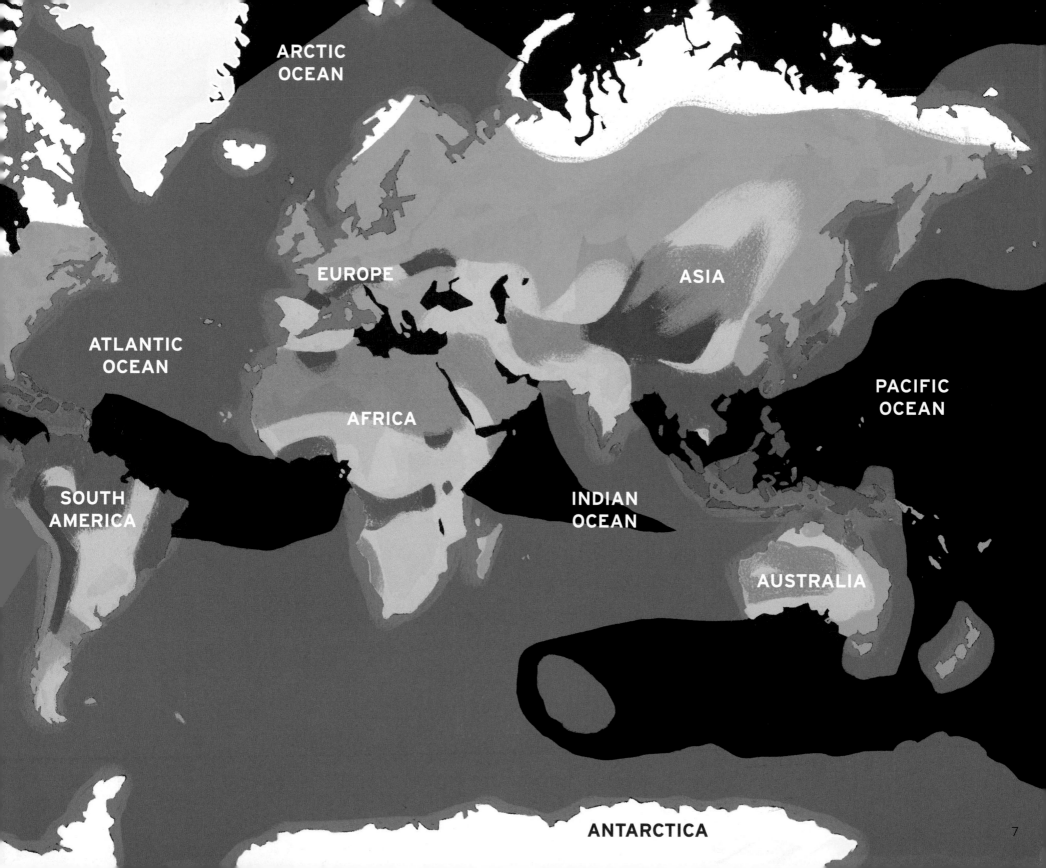

ARCTIC
OCEAN

EUROPE

ASIA

ATLANTIC
OCEAN

PACIFIC
OCEAN

AFRICA

SOUTH
AMERICA

INDIAN
OCEAN

AUSTRALIA

ANTARCTICA

Chapter 1

BEYOND BLACK AND WHITE

It's June off the coast of San Juan Island, and three Southern Resident orca whales—L-113 (Cousteau), L-25 (Ocean Sun), and L-41 (Mega)—swim past a nineteen-foot boat, breathing in unison. Drifting puffy clouds cast gray shadows on the surface of the sea, making it hard to distinguish between a whale's black fin and the water. Lingering in the orcas' wake is a thick, salty bitterness that clings to the air and latches on to the tip of your tongue. Ken Balcomb isn't fazed by the elements; he's on a mission to keep track of these endangered whales. From May until October, or for as long as the whales decide to stay, Ken and his crew from the Center for Whale Research (CWR) regularly track the Southern Residents and take note of who's swimming with whom.

By midmorning, the fog begins to melt away into a clearer sky. In the palm of his hand Ken cradles a 400-mm lens and looks through his camera's viewfinder. Photo identification is a game that involves rushing, observing, and waiting for the perfect shot. All three whales travel up and over the waves as Ken balances on deck. *Steady, steady, shoot.* His goal by the first week of July is to photograph all eighty-three Southern Resident whale fins and add them to his annual field guide. Many scientists, including several at the National Oceanic Atmospheric Administration (NOAA) in Seattle, will use this database for future studies.

L-41 (Mega) is easily spotted by his unique dorsal fin. He is often seen with L-77 (Matia), her daughter L-119 (Joy), and L-85 (Mystery). Mystery, pictured in the far back, lost his mother at the age of three but stays close to his family even at age twenty-six.

Photographs of every Southern Resident whale allow Ken to identify "who's who" in each pod.

The three whales disappear beneath the surface as another whale catches Ken's attention. It's J-28 (Polaris) alongside her second calf, J-54 (Dipper). Their blow explodes and sounds out *kaawoof, kaawoof*. A stream of blow shoots into the air like a fountain. Polaris is as big as the boat, and she's built to command the sea. With a flick of her fluke or a body roll, she's capable of capsizing the boat, and Ken with it. However, she has no time for such behavior. Badgering boats is not her style. It's not the style of any Southern Resident, for that matter. They have bigger matters to tend to, starting with their appetites. It's surprising that they're often referred to as "killer whales." In forty years, Ken's never seen a Southern Resident kill anything other than a fish. As Polaris swims, her fellow pod members dive under boats and kayaks and travel in the direction of the fish they're pursuing. Over the years, she and her ancestors have learned to adapt to the changes of less food and busier waterways. Ken clicks the shutter button to get her telltale nicked fin on record. Polaris is the forty-third Southern Resident whale fin he's captured on film this season.

Every year, new "mug shots" are added to the CWR field guide. This collection of photographs is a cross between a family album and an orca yearbook. Ken can identify each whale by its fin. Many people in the local community identify the Southern Resident whales by the nicknames given to them by the Whale Museum in Friday Harbor, Washington. Once a new calf becomes a year old, a naming contest begins in which museum members submit their favorite names for new calves born that year. Staff members at the Whale Museum select the finalists, and the public gets a vote. Not all whales get their names this way. Whale calves born to the J-14 (Samish) matriline—or "mother line"—are given a special ceremony. (To learn more about the Samish naming ceremony, see the sidebar on page 21.)

As popular as the whales' nicknames are, Ken doesn't know the Southern Residents by these names. Instead, he and other scientists refer to each whale by a letter and number, the system started by Mike Bigg in the 1970s. The letter represents the pod, and the number indicates the birth order of the whale. Ken can identify every individual by this alphanumeric classification. He believes that the whales can identify him as well.

On occasion, he says, some whales come over to inspect him while showing him their new calves: "Obviously they can tell the sound of our boat. Even if other boats are around, they come to us as if to say, 'You're here again!'" On other occasions, Ken's been visited by bulls, or adult males, coming right up to his boat. When he peers down over the side, the bull stares up at him. Often the two will lock eyes until the bull decides to swim away. There's no mistaking curiosity is an indication of the depth of the orcas' intelligence. Science necropsies show that the large brain of an orca contains cortical thickness, a physical trait associated with consciousness, memory, attention, language, and thought.

The L pod swims near Ken as he photographs.

In the past, when salmon were plentiful, superpods were seen often.

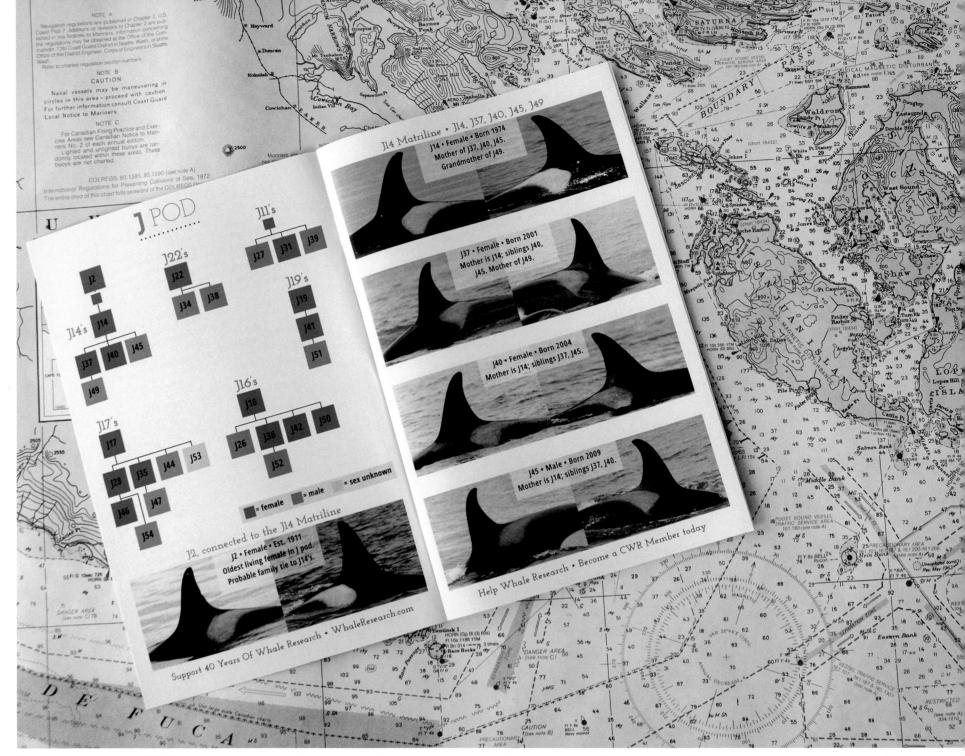

Every year, a new CWR catalog shows each member of the Southern Resident pod and links each individual to its family tree. Information collected in long-term studies by the Center for Whale Research is used to better understand and protect the whales in both Canada and the United States.

Saddle patches are like fingerprints. Ken compares photos of J-28 (Polaris) over time and sees that her saddle patch design remains the same.

J-28 (Polaris) is identified by her signature saddle patch and dorsal fin notch.

Because the Southern Residents are predators, they eat often throughout their typical seventy-five-mile-a-day journey around the Salish Sea. The Southern Resident whales' main source of food is salmon, specifically Chinook salmon. The Fraser River watershed is the largest Canadian producer of Chinook salmon, and the Fraser River Chinook are actually divided into four "stocks," or subspecies. Each subspecies migrates from different areas, depending on the season. The Chinook stock comes from a different geographical area on the Fraser River, which runs through Canadian waters and empties into the tip of the Georgia Strait, also called the Salish Sea. This U.S. waterway is the Southern Residents' summer habitat. It's believed that each whale eats about 5 percent of its body weight in fish each day.

In recent years, Ken and other scientists have seen how low numbers of salmon are creating problems for the Southern Residents. Specifically, in search of fish, these whales are traveling greater distances from routes they took in previous years. This lessens the time when they can socialize, play, and rest. Food is at the center of their world. In years past, when food was plentiful, one could often observe greeting ceremonies, known as superpods, where whales from the J, K, and L pods form two lines about sixty-five yards (59 meters) apart and swim toward one another. When they meet, they roll around and touch. Ken describes this as equivalent to people running toward each other and embracing in a hug, lifting each other in the air, and jumping up and down. For Southern Residents, it's social interaction that can last for thirty minutes. When they're done, the whales typically head off to travel in the same direction. There have been fewer superpod encounters in recent years, but Ken remembers them well: "From our point of view, it gives a feeling that they're really having a nice time getting together." With the whales spreading out farther away from their family members in search of food, it's becoming increasingly difficult to locate the residents on any given day. As Ken describes it, "Everybody can't be at the picnic table if there isn't any food. If there's

It's a family affair. Siblings J-46 (Star) and J-54 (Dipper) swim with their mom, J-28 (Polaris).

food, they'll all be there." Because of this, he is making a more concerted effort to find the whales as they travel farther north.

Back on deck and off to the west, the crew watches as Polaris strays farther from her family, leaving her first offspring, the preadolescent J-46 (Star) to fend for herself. The added freedom from her mom gives this growing calf the opportunity to play and socialize among other whales. Even though Polaris wanders a bit with her newest calf, Dipper, she won't stray too far from Star. Resident whales such as the Southern Residents seem to see their family as everything. They're known to be the most family-oriented subspecies of orca in the world. They swim, hunt, and play with Mom, Grandma, aunts, and uncles—for life. Mothers nurse their calves for seven to eight months before weaning them. Young calves stick to their moms like magnets. Ken believes this constant care is a true testament to their commitment to one another.

Swimming slightly east, leading the pod, is J-17 (Princess Angeline). She's the oldest female in this particular group, and as a grandma, she's held in high regard by her family members, who are always in her presence. When the whales are still, and Ken is not shooting photos, he listens. He can hear their distant underwater sounds of squeaks and whistles from ten feet away. It's the orcas communicating and socializing. Different pods have different dialects that can be heard more clearly with the special underwater equipment. Each pod's dialect is similar, with subtle differences specific to certain families. Ken attributes this similarity to the accents of people in New Jersey versus those in Washington State speaking the same language. As Princess Angeline swims, she's almost always communicating. Everyone in the pod listens, including young Star. It's taken years for Star to learn to make the sounds of her pod. Someday, when she has a calf, she'll pass on all she knows.

As the pod heads south, Princess Angeline rockets out of the water like a gymnast, twisting her body. She's breaching. With massive force, she drops back to the water's surface. A splash bursts, spraying water in every direction. Ken captures this with his camera. "She's who I call the acrobat of the bunch. I can always find her jumping or slapping the water at some point," he says. Princess Angeline's son, J-44 (Moby), steers to her right about a hundred yards (91 meters) away. Moby, like all Southern Resident males, stays closer to his mom than any of his sisters do. Several scientists refer to Southern Resident males as "mama's boys."

Loud *chufffff*s echo along with the sound of Ken's camera shutter. He pushes the button, and the camera clicks. *Ka-chick, ka-chick, ka-chick, ka-chick*. After Star comes up for a breath, she rounds her back along the surface, leaving just enough time for Ken to capture a photo of her saddle patch, which looks like an exaggerated comma. Two juvenile males, J-51 (Nova) and J-47 (Notch), swim beside Star. Notch is named for a notch nicked on his dorsal fin. In between foraging and traveling, these two young males frolic and curl their bodies over the waves and each other, which can often result in raking, or tooth marks, on the side of a whale. This is common among young male and female whales, but not all of them partake in this behavior. Ken also uses rake marks to identify the whales. From his perspective, "The whales don't have hands, and they do a lot of touching. The way they can hold on to something is by biting. It's kind of like saying, 'Hey, buddy-buddy' and then grabbing on."

After about fifteen minutes the J pod whales move out of range. Ken feels his cell phone vibrate in his pocket. Every time a whale is spotted, he receives a text from the ship captains in the area. "Looks like we've got some Ks far off, about ten miles [16,093 meters] from Victoria," Ken says. "They seem to be foraging west." Victoria is close to the ninety-five-mile (15,288-meter) stretch to the Pacific Ocean known as the Strait of Juan de Fuca. Here, the sea chop is strong and the ride is rough. Ken knows that whales frequent these waters, but he's hesitant to go there with a forecast of worsening weather. He cranks up the engine and circles his way back to CWR, the boat slamming against the water at high speed. Ken tucks his white beard under his neck warmer and stays bundled beneath a heavy-duty plaid jacket. Today, upon his return to CWR, he and the staff will add the photos to the identification database. Through-

J-17 (Princess Angeline) is perhaps best known for her acrobatics including belly flops as pictured here.

out the rest of the summer and into the fall they'll take note of any births, deaths, or health concerns they observe.

Unfortunately, there's no time to waste. The Southern Resident population is struggling through the aftermath of years of marine park captures, lack of food, environmental issues, and toxins in the water, all factors that are putting them at risk. For all the problems humans have created to interfere in the world of the Southern Residents, Ken says, "The orcas have no malice toward humans, or anything that I've seen, and we owe it to them to protect them."

In 2005, after about ten years of a steady decline, the whale population dropped from one hundred to eighty. In response to this noticeable decline, Ken alerted NOAA. A year later, a plan was put in place to examine the factors affecting these whales. Southern Residents are now listed as an endangered species, and studies are still underway. Ken and several other scientists are working together in a full-on investigation in an effort to help save the Southern Resident orca whales from extinction.

It's his hope that if we pay close attention to the whales and the changes going on in their world, things will get better. It's a hope that will help not only the future of the whales, but ours as well. Ken remains optimistic, and he's looking forward to that day when the whales all come together to share in a feast and perhaps another greeting ceremony. Until then, he'll continue to keep track. It's the least he can do for a group of whales he calls family.

J pod members J-17 (Princess Angeline), her daughter J-35 (Tahlequah) and son J-44 (Moby) swim away.

J-51 (Nova) and J-47 (Notch) frolic. Frolicking is typical behavior among juvenile whales.

WHY ARE ORCAS BLACK AND WHITE?

Orcas have a distinctive pattern of black and white, and scientists believe this serves as a form of camouflage from their prey. As the whales swim, their light-colored undersides make them less visible in the water. In contrast, their black tops make them hard to distinguish in the midst of dark water surroundings. Having black-and-white coloration also helps break up the image of the large body size of the whales. This comes in handy for the whales when they are hunting and sneaking up on their prey.

MALE AND FEMALE

• Orcas are the largest members of the dolphin family.
• Males are larger than females, with taller dorsal fins.
• By their twenty-fifth birthday males grow to an average of twenty to twenty-six feet (6 to 8 meters) and weigh in the range of eight to twelve thousand pounds (3,600 to 5,400 kilograms).
• By the time the females are fifteen years old, they become mature and grow to an average of sixteen to twenty-three feet (5 to 7 meters) and weigh in the range of three thousand to six thousand pounds (1,300 to 2,700 kilograms).
• Females live an average of fifty years, though some individuals have lived as long as eighty to one hundred years.
• Males live an average of twenty-nine years, and some have lived as long as fifty to sixty years.
• Mating takes place all year long.

SOUTHERN RESIDENT ORCA CALVES

• Calves weigh on average four hundred pounds at birth (180 kilograms) and are generally seven to eight feet long (2 to 3 meters).
• Gestation, or pregnancy, varies from fifteen to eighteen months, and the average birthing rate is one calf every five years.
• Calves typically nurse until they are two years old, and they begin eating solid food at one year.
• Currently, the youngest known Southern Resident mother is J-41 (Eclipse), who had her first calf, J-51 (Nova), at age eleven.

dorsal fin

saddle patch

blowhole

eyespot

fluke

pectoral fins

J-46 (Star) is identified by her saddle patch, which resembles an exaggerated comma.

The three-year-old J-50 (Scarlet) was spotted after her birth with a set of rake marks brought on by family members using their teeth as a way to assist in a difficult delivery.

L-25 (Ocean Sun) is identified by a saddle patch that resembles a hook.

Rake marks on the two-year-old male J-52 (Sonic) are from frolicking with other juvenile Southern Residents.

THE SAMISH INDIAN NATION'S NAMING CEREMONY

A man walks with his handmade painted drum and beats to the rhythm of a steady thump. He and others from the Samish Indian Nation gather beside the sea. A Samish Nation child stops when he reaches the four blankets that cover the floor. All are present in celebration of the newly born Southern Resident calf.

Every whale calf related to the female whale J-14 (Samish) is honored in a naming ceremony like this. The name Samish was chosen for J-14 by the Whale Museum in Friday Harbor; it was selected as a tribute to the Samish Nation culture, which believes that J pod members like Samish are their ancestors. Guests from the Whale Museum are invited as "witnesses" to attend ceremonies such as this and are asked to pass on what's seen and heard to others in the community. The Whale Museum advocates for the safety and health of the Southern Resident whales and because of this, the Samish Nation holds the museum in high regard. Pacific Northwest Native Americans' stories and rituals relating to orca whales date back thousands of years. The connection between orcas and natives is strong among many tribal cultures to this day.

As the ceremony progresses, Samish drummers and singers chant melodies as they follow behind the child, who moves through the crowd holding the whale calf's image up high. The newly named whale is announced to all those in attendance.

The Samish Nation partakes in many ceremonies related to Southern Residents. Rosie Cayou, Bill Bailey, and Kelly Hall sing in honor of J-14 (Samish).

Chapter 2

BEST CATCH OF THE DAY

"The kid must have something. The way they're acting is very suspicious," says the biologist Candi Emmons. To the left of the boat, near the outboard, a Chinook salmon jumps nearly half an arm's length out of the water. When it plunges back beneath the surface, eleven-year-old J-41 (Eclipse) and her one-and-a-half-year-old son, J-51 (Nova), are now within twenty yards, or sixty feet, of the boat. Candi and Dr. Brad Hanson, also a biologist, watch as the scene unfolds. Eclipse swims to the fish, clips it in her jaw, and then lets it go. On the opposite side, Nova chases the fish, clenches it in his sharp teeth, then loses his grip. Eclipse makes a small turn and swims sideways. White streaks on her underbelly stream through the water; she's close enough to touch. In a quick second, she lunges down to the back of the boat, where the salmon is hiding under the motor. With a quick *pop* she hits the fish with her head as if to stun it. The two whales corkscrew beneath the boat and pursue the fish. Eclipse corrals the stunned salmon, moving it closer to her son, who grabs it and bites down; the salmon seems to be the length of a yardstick.

Nova is learning how to hunt from his young mom. The chase, packed with speed and efficiency, lasts nearly three minutes. The two swim away, sharing their fresh catch. As mom and calf swim past the boat one last time, Candi says, "Good mom, J-forty-one! You did a

NOAA team members skimming in the wake of leftover whale scraps.

J-41 (Eclipse) shares fish with her recently weaned calf, J-51 (Nova), after she teaches him how to hunt. Fish sharing is a common practice in the Southern Resident community.

great job." Eclipse's mom, J-19 (Sachi), taught her this behavior years ago and now the tradition is carrying on with Nova, as it has for thousands of years.

Brad, Candi, and their marine biology intern Robert don puffy red nylon jumpsuits that make them look a lot like astronauts. The suits work as full-body life preservers and fit neatly over their clothing to keep them warm and protected from splashing seawater. Candi kicks the engine back on, and the small inflatable boat coasts slowly. The team of scientists hangs back at a distance, far from the departing whales. From the bow, Brad keeps a vigilant eye out for floating blobs of fish pieces left over from the hunt. They're hoping to gather the fish scraps that have scales; fish scales tell the biologists what type of fish the whales eat. The scales also indicate which rivers the fish are from. Evidence suggests that Chinook salmon are the Southern

Residents' favorite prey. Brad's goal is to understand the potential impact the prey have on the overall health of the Southern Residents.

Suddenly Brad shouts, *"Scaaales!"* Candi steers based on Brad's navigation calls. "Off to the right, more to the right, right—stop." Brad collects the scales to later analyze their DNA. This analysis will tell him which Chinook salmon subpopulation the whales are eating and the type of Chinook they depend on the most. He leans over the platform anchored over the center of the bow and reaches forward, catching his balance by rocking along with the rolling waves that seemingly come from nowhere. Candi shifts the gears into idle and steps away from the boat's steering wheel. As the white, fleshy blob of fish drifts closer, Brad dips an eighteen-foot (5.5-meter) pole—which has an attached swimming pool net—underneath the morsel. To Brad, an array of different sample types is key: "My approach is that we have several questions to address, and almost every sample type has some bias, so you look at multiple approaches to get at that question."

Candi unhooks the ocean-drenched net from Brad's pole and passes it to Robert, who takes it and parks himself in the back of the boat. The net is crawling with tan-colored critters that look like a circle of ice. These are tiny white comb jellyfish known as ctenophores, and they're mixed in with a smattering of fish chunks and scales. Next to Robert is a gray box filled with the field tools he needs: a snack-size

plastic bag, forceps, and a black marker. He examines the net, tweezing fish scales that have anchored themselves in the mesh, holding the net closer to his face to get a better view. He separates the jellies from the scales, then peels the jellies and throws them back into the water. Lastly, he places the scales in a plastic bag, to be put on ice. For the next thirty minutes, Brad and Candi look for more samples while Robert turns his lap into a workstation.

Brad skims then dips the net under the surface to lift the fish scraps.

Tiny comb jellies are common in Washington State waters and get stuck in the net along with the scales.

Fish scales are picked off the net with tweezers.

Robert uses a GoPro camera to watch the whales hunting for Chinook salmon underwater.

As Candi steers, she points toward a ripple on the water and increases the speed to fifteen miles (24 kilometers) per hour. "There's something out there," she says. When the boat slows, she and Brad take a look at a floating fish head. "That's not something we want, is it . . . a fish head?" Candi asks Brad. Looking at it up close, Brad identifies it as the head of a cod. "Forget it," he says. This fish head isn't what he's after; it's not the head of a salmon and was likely left behind by something other than a Southern Resident.

The team motors on, also looking for whales that haven't been biopsied for a blubber sample in more than a year. In no time, a pod of Southern Residents swims past. Candi identifies a whale, then looks at her chart to see who is due for a biopsy. Brad switches out his pole and net to take a sample with a dart gun. Biopsies can show what's going on inside the whale and will verify the whale's DNA to determine who its parents are. It will also indicate which contaminants are present. Over the next several years, before this portion of the study is complete, an attempt will be made to dart every Southern Resident.

By taking a health assessment of each Southern Resident whale, the scientists will be able to narrow down the specific issues that are putting this population at risk. "Just because animals look healthy doesn't mean they are. They mask it," Brad says. "What we're concerned about is that if we don't keep track of what's going on, some of the animals may just up and die."

Candi spots a male to her left. "Ha, and out of nowhere comes L-eighty-seven [Onyx]. He's always everywhere and nowhere," she jokes. Only a handful of scientists can identify every whale by sight the way Ken can. Candi's one of them. When she first started in the field, she did photo identification work with Ken, and she remembers spending endless hours learning about the physical characteristics that set each Southern Resident apart. Now she uses this skill to help Brad.

Brad's excitement grows when he spots three fluke or tail prints lingering on the surface. This smooth patch is what a whale leaves when it flicks its fluke in an upward, then downward motion. Often this movement is followed by a piece of floating scat—otherwise known as poop. Brad collects it when possible to pass on to other scientists who analyze it. As the boat motors closer, much to the scientists' dismay, there's no scat to be found. Candi describes this as a typical day: "You usually get eating days and poop days; you rarely get both."

In two weeks, Brad and Candi have collected a total of three full biopsy samples, fifteen fecal samples, and three fish scale sample bags. It's a good start, but they're hoping for more. Each sample type plays an important role. In the fall, they'll return for another few weeks and hopefully more whale encounters.

At the day's end, the team starts heading back. It's 8:00 p.m., and the sun will be falling fast. J-16 (Slick), her young-

A fluke print left in an orca's wake is a good indicator of scat coming soon.

The family of L-87 (Onyx) consists of his sister L-22 (Spirit), her adult offspring L-89 (Solstice), and his cousin L-85 (Mystery).

est offspring, J-50 (Scarlet), and daughter J-42 (Echo) slow their speed and rest at the surface. Slick's older offspring—J-36 (Alki), J-26 (Mike), and J-52 (Sonic)—eventually meet up with them to rest. Glistening black dorsal fins point to the sky in a standstill. As today's journey ends, the scientists' mission to gather samples from the whales has also come to a standstill, at least until tomorrow.

Candi uses the CWR annual catalog to identify Southern Residents.

The NOAA crew watch the J pod members resting. When whales rest, they often come together abreast in a tight group, moving extremely slowly in a forward direction for long periods while at the surface.

The blubber sample offers an inside look into the health of a whale.

ORCA FOOD AROUND THE WORLD

- *Transient whales of Washington State eat marine mammals, mainly seals and sea lions. All transient orcas are sneaky, daring, and powerful in their attacks.*

- *Transient whales in British Columbia are known to be the true "killer of whales." Minke whales, as well as fin whales and humpback whales, are often seen being killed by these transient groups. British Columbia transients are also known to prey upon Dall's porpoises and harbor porpoises.*

- *Transients in California are frequently seen feeding on gray whale calves.*

- *Both Northern and Southern Resident whales in Washington State and Vancouver are known to be salmon specialists. Northern Residents vary their diet a bit more by feeding on squid, lingcod, and halibut.*

- *Offshore species of orca found along the continental shelf feed on sleeper sharks.*

- *New Zealand orcas feed on mako sharks and stingrays.*

- *Some orcas in Patagonia, Argentina, patrol up and down at the edge of the beach in search of sea lions, then charge the beach to grab the sea lion pup in their mouths. Crozet Islands orcas that inhabit the southern Indian Ocean do the same. Crozet orcas also feed on penguins.*

- *New Zealand orcas off Kaikoura feed on dusky dolphins.*

- *Antarctic orcas are clever hunters that spy-hop around ice floes to get a good view of seals that they can push into the water.*

- *Off the Norwegian coast, orcas prey on the huge schools of herring.*

It's late June when Brad finishes collecting scales and blubber and heads back to NOAA's lab in Seattle with a variety of data to analyze. He places the samples in a freezer at -80°F (-62°C) until it's time for analysis. At the lab, the research chemist Gina Ylitalo has enough samples to draw some conclusions. She cautiously unwraps the foil from the blubber biopsies, saying, "They're worth their weight in gold—and then some." A lot of information is stored in a piece of fat and Gina rations off a part of this small sample for genetic testing and other types of analysis to be done at a later date. At the moment, she's interested in finding contaminants in the blubber. First she cuts the sample in half lengthwise, a technique that takes precision. She then passes it to her lab colleagues, who begin the analysis. They'll be working with a batch of thirteen samples at a time, and to get the process started, it's all about separating the contaminants from fats and chemical elements that could interfere with measurements.

Upon his return to NOAA in Seattle, Brad freezes samples until they're needed for analysis.

The samples go into a container mixed with drying agents to remove any water, and the mixture is then packed into an extraction cell that will hold it in place. There's very little room to wiggle inside this cell. The chemists add a solvent that helps to extract or separate contaminants from the sample. Once the machine finishes this process, known as extraction, it's time for a cleanup. When the chemists at NOAA clean, they take their time. Unfortunately for those anxiously waiting answers, "It takes a *long* time," Gina says. Five days, to be exact.

Gina has enough samples to begin an analysis worthy of producing conclusions.

After a thorough cleaning, the chemists are left with an extract of only one milliliter (ml). There are about five milliliters in one teaspoon of sugar. That means Gina's sample is as small as dividing a teaspoon of sugar into five parts and taking only one of those parts—a very small sample size. Nonetheless, Gina uses this measurement to make calculations. When the process is complete, the blubber biopsies reveal that the Southern Resident whales have extremely high contaminant levels. In other words, there are chemicals in the orcas' bodies.

Some of these chemicals, such as polychlorinated biphenyls (PCBs) and dichlorodiphenyltrichloroethane (DDTs), date back to the 1920s. PCBs were used as a coolant for industrial machines. DDTs were used as an insecticide for agricultural purposes. Both chemicals were released into the marine en-

Blubber samples are considered "scientific gold."

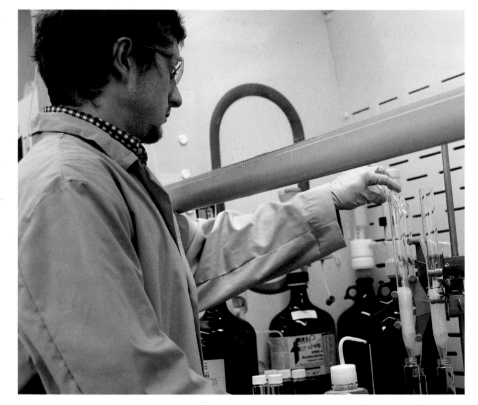

The chemist adds solvent to the samples.

vironment, and they remain there. Although they have been banned since the 1970s, they still show up in Pacific Northwest resident and transient orcas. Marine animals such as whales ingest these chemicals and store them in their fatty deposits. "The whales don't have gills or feed on sediment on the ocean floor; it's most likely that they're ingesting these chemicals through the fish they eat," says Gina.

Upon further analysis, Gina also finds high levels of polybrominated diphenyl ether flame retardants (PBDEs) in the blubber samples. PBDEs, once used to protect items from catching fire, were banned in 2004. New furniture, mattresses, and pajamas, among other things, were coated with this compound. Gina combines the information from this data with the results of the genetic tests that come back from an adjacent NOAA lab. Genetics help Gina determine which of the blubber samples are from males and which are from females. With this information she is able to compare the contaminant load in male and female orcas that are close in age.

Weeks later, when Gina, Brad, Candi, and others at NOAA meet to discuss the results, they find that male orcas accumulate contaminants steadily throughout their lives. In contrast, samples reveal that levels of DDTs, PBDEs, and PCBs increase in females until they reproduce. Unfortunately, when a female becomes pregnant, these toxic chemicals are passed to the fetus while it is in the womb. After a calf is born, the chemicals are again passed through its mother's milk. Examining the blubber samples reveals that there are higher levels of contaminants in the calves than in their mothers. To the scientists, this makes perfect sense. Orca milk is approximately 70 percent fat and comes from the orcas' fat stores. This means that orca babies get a sizable dose of PCBs and DDT with every meal. These chemicals are absorbed into the animal's body and stored in its blubber. For the young Southern Resident orcas, this may contribute to the high infant mortality rate within the population.

The contaminant levels indicate that when the whales are exposed to these chemicals, their bodies store them in fat within their blubber layer. Without an adequate amount of prey to feed on, the whales may need to use the fat reserves in their blubber as an energy source. At this point these chemicals are transported throughout the body and weaken the whale's immune system.

As pieces of the Southern Resident recovery puzzle are put together, it's becoming clearer with each finding that an abundant and viable fish source plays a pivotal role in the Southern Resident orca recovery. Gina and her colleagues continue looking at the samples as they come into the lab. "They're invaluable. You just never know when you'll see them again. Some are pretty old animals. We're all trying to get as much information as we can."

Gina uses the 1.0 milliliter sample to make calculations; then the samples go inside the extraction cell.

J-2 (Granny) (in the lead) is an identified member of the focal follow; she's followed for up to thirty minutes.

Chapter 3

PUMP UP THE VOLUME

The whales in the J, K, and L pods are extremely active. They're often observed in vibrant and enthusiastic displays involving jumps, slaps, and cartwheels. The whales seem to perform these behaviors—known as surface-active behaviors (SABs)—everywhere and out of nowhere. These performances are entertaining to anyone fortunate enough to see them, and when the scientist Dr. Dawn Noren watches, she pays careful attention.

More than ten years ago, in 2005, Dawn traveled from NOAA in Seattle to the San Juan Islands to determine whether these displays changed when the whales were in the presence of vessels or boats. To get the job done right, Dawn worked throughout the summer months for two consecutive years. She and her team used the focal follow approach, a pretty straight-forward concept that is tried and true among field biologists. First she became familiar with each whale's identifiable characteristics. When she found a whale, she'd watch it without letting it out of her sight for up to thirty minutes. Her field assistant Erin recorded the number of vessels present, if any. Several times, Dawn followed J-2 (Granny), the oldest living Southern Resident. Surprisingly, Dawn found that Granny's senior status wasn't going to slow her down anytime soon. Granny, a seemingly popular whale, was typically found swimming in the lead of other J pod members. Often, Dawn observed Granny lifting her tail out of the water and

Pectoral slap

Tail slap

K-20 breach

Cartwheel

Spy hop

slamming it down with a single splash. Every time Granny performed this behavior during a focal follow, Dawn clicked her PalmPilot device under the behavior name "tail slap." At one point she observed Granny performing seven tail slaps over an eight-second time period. Scientists have long believed that tail slaps are used as a form of communication within a pod. Dawn was eager to find out if more slaps occurred when vessels approached (even though she wasn't exactly sure what Granny was telling the rest of the pod when she slapped).

On other occasions Dawn observed J-1 (Ruffles), a male who typically swam in close proximity to Granny. Dawn watched as the whale, between his regular swimming behavior, performed a breach with three vessels present. Dawn tapped "breach" on the screen, and Erin recorded the number of vessels present. Other times Dawn identified J-26 (Mike)—named after the late Dr. Mike Bigg. She would watch him perform a series of exaggerated tail slaps, known as "cartwheels." In a cartwheel, Mike hurled the bottom part of his body up out of the water and over his head.

During the next several months, Dawn recorded six types of SABs. When a whale slapped the water with its dorsal fin and rolled on its side, it was doing a "dorsal slap." Other behaviors included a "pectoral slap"—a slap of the whale's pectoral fin on the water—and a "spy hop," when a whale lifts its head vertically out of the water, with both eyes exposed. Not all whales could be followed for the full thirty minutes. In these cases, Dawn said, "My cutoff for including data in the analysis is ten minutes of continuous data collection, even though we aimed for thirty minutes."

J-26 (Mike)

At the time of this study, J-1 (Ruffles), nicknamed for his ruffled dorsal fin, and J-2 (Granny) were typically seen traveling together.

At the end of this two-year study, Dawn had nearly 370 focal follows of 45 individual Southern Resident whales. Perhaps the most telling data of all indicated that Granny had chronic tail-slapping behavior and regularly performed several tail-slaps in a row when in the presence of vessels. Dawn believed that tail-slaps were used as a form of communication and as a response to close-approaching vessels. "For the most part," Dawn said, "there was an indication that the focal follow whales perform more SAB activity at the surface when boats are closer to them." She found that the highest number of SABs occurred when a vessel approached a Southern Resident whale. More specifically, data showed that the highest number of SABs was performed when whales were within 150 meters (492 feet) of a boat.

While at NOAA, Dawn reviews the focal follow data of forty-five whales. Data analysis indicates that more bouts of SABs occur when vessels are near the Southern Residents.

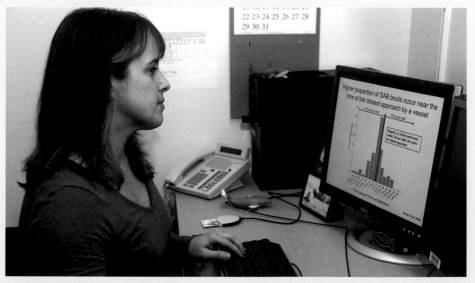

Now that the research confirmed that vessel traffic affected the whales' behavior, another scientist, Dr. Marla Holt, wondered if added traffic noise required the whales to "pump up their volume" in order to be heard. In 2007, a year after Dawn's findings, Marla decided that the next logical step would be to investigate the whale sounds—referred to as acoustic behavior. It would take a few weeks in the field to find the answers, and because this would require more than one person, Marla asked Dawn to come onboard. While Marla listened, Dawn documented whale behavior and the number of vessels within 3,281 feet (1,000 meters) of the whales.

Marla hooked up her computer laptop to a pair of headphones and a hydrophone, or underwater microphone. Through an amplifier and recorder, whale sounds were converted to visual form on the laptop screen. When Marla dropped the hydrophone into the water beside the boat, the cord stretched to about sixteen feet (5 meters) below the surface. Within an instant the hydrophone picked up a symphony of sounds. It was the whales talking to one another through a complex variety of calls, whines, whistles, and squeaks. Marla also heard faint *snaps*, *pops*, and *clicks*, all part of the whales' echolocation, which they use to find food. Whales make these and other noises with the air trapped in their nasal passage, and it comes out as sound when it travels through their forehead.

At first, Marla heard a noise similar to the sound a cloth

Southern Residents perform fewer SABs when vessels keep a distance of about five hundred feet (150 meters) or more.

makes wiping down a window with glass cleaner: *reee-ong, reee-ong, ree-ong*. This was the L-12 matriline's signature sound, known to be the S2iii call. S2iii and other calls are used by the offspring of female L-12 as a signal to tell others in the pod where they are located as well as what's going on in the area. L-12 is deceased, yet her signature call carries on through her family. The thirty-year-old female L-22 (Spirit) swam close to her fourteen-year-old son, L-89 (Solstice), and twenty-year-old L-77 (Matia). These three are members of the L-12 matriline and can regularly be seen traveling together in a larger group of eight. As they swam,

Marla deploys the hydrophone; the digital device converts the sounds to a visual on screen.

their sounds acted as an acoustic lens that helped them navigate, socialize, and find food. There were many different calls or dialects, depending on a pod's matriline. In the midst of burbles, squeals, whistles, raspberries, and snorts, Marla focused on recording one call in particular—the S1 call, common among all three pods.

When members of the J pod swam past, Marla recorded the calls and background noises of J-16 (Slick) and J-42 (Echo) on a recording device. Beside her, Dawn pointed her laser range finder at a nearby boat. The whale voices sounded out and repeated *weeeoowup, waaawaaawp, whoooeee*— the typical S1 "rusty door hinge" sound coming through. In addition to echolocation clicks, these piercingly loud calls were the sounds the whales make in their pursuit to find salmon. Although scientists aren't really sure what this universal call translates to in terms of human language, Marla

Upon analysis at NOAA, Marla looks at different colors in sound waves, indicating increased frequency.

A visual image of the S2iii sound made by the L-12 matriline. Even though L-12 has passed away, her family continues to use this call, which is unique to their pod.

A visual image of the signature S1 sound.

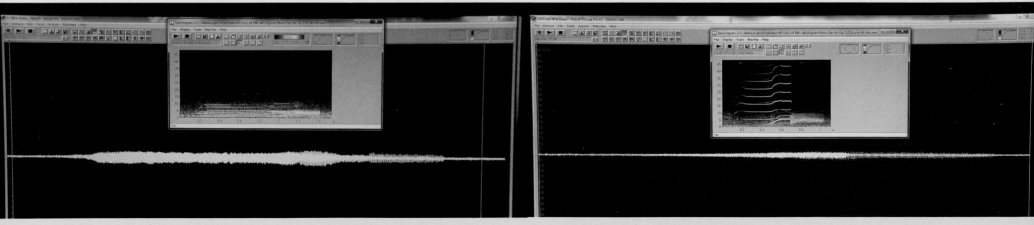

said, "it could be compared to you calling 'Hey' to your mom as a way of letting her know where you are and that you're okay." Marla hit the record button on the spectrogram to see a colorful line of vibrations on the computer screen indicating the sounds she heard over the headphones. This rainbow of sound decorated the screen in waves. With each click of the button, the spectrogram recorded this "voice-print." Marla realized that the waves were darker in color when they were near the vessels. This indicated that the Southern Residents increased their S1 call when they were near vessels. Interestingly, Marla found that as boat noises go up by one decibel, so did the whales' S1 call. Once again, it was clear that Southern Resident whale behavior changed when in the presence of boats.

In 2011, federal officials and lawmakers took note of the various studies, including Dawn and Marla's, and enacted changes necessary to protect the whales from vessels getting too close. This safety measure mandates distance requirements between whales and vessels. More distance from the whales is likely to minimize disruption in routine behaviors, including foraging. As a result, under federal law, vessels and kayaks need to stay at least six hundred feet (183 meters) from a Southern Resident whale at all times. This is one component of the Southern Resident recovery plan that's been implemented into law.

Dawn demonstrates how a laser range finder is used in the field.

These preliminary studies laid the foundation for much of Dawn and Marla's research in years to follow. As Dawn says, "The cool thing about fieldwork is that you have this major question, but then, depending on the data you collect, you can formulate a lot of different questions." With that, both scientists still continued to wonder: Could added vessel traffic around the Southern Residents mean more energy spent raising the volume of their calls and less time feeding? Finding the answer to this remained a mystery, especially as it was virtually impossible to measure how much energy wild orcas use in different scenarios. Luckily, these scientists weren't going to stop at the impossible. That's when they decided to introduce themselves to the world of Primo and Puka, two bottle-nosed dolphins.

Primo and Puka are trained and retired U.S. Navy dolphins, now at Dr. Terrie Williams's lab at the University of California, Santa Cruz. Since bottle-nosed dolphins are close relatives to orcas, scientists use captive animals like Primo and Puka to answer difficult questions in relation to their wild counterparts. Previous studies show that orcas and bottle-nosed dolphins both produce different varieties of whistle sounds when communicating. Whistles are social sounds used in communication. Now it was time to look at the energy used to produce these sounds.

It's midwinter, and Primo begins his morning by watching the signals of his animal trainer, Beau. In one hand Beau holds a soft rubber suction cup. Embedded in this soft rubber cup is a sand-dollar–size hydrophone that records all of Primo's sounds. Beau signals for Primo to swim to a dome that's sitting on top of the water. Basically, the dome is a modified skylight that the dolphin parks itself under when asked. Here, Primo remains still, allowing Beau to secure the suction cup on his forehead. Next, Beau raises his hand, Primo starts to make some noise, producing a whistle sound, and the hydrophone on his forehead records each whistle: *Weeoouu, weeoouu, weeoouu.* Primo continues to repeat this sound until Beau blows his own whistle.

K-35 (Sonata) calls louder and breaches more in the presence of vessels. For future studies, especially as new pipelines are built and oil shipping traffic increases, scientists will explore ways to establish critical habitat where the Southern Residents reside.

Primo at the University of California, Santa Cruz

Trainer Beau watches Primo while under the dome.

This means "stop." Primo's only movement comes from his breath while he stays still. When he breathes, air samples are pulled through a blue pool-vacuum hose attached to the dome. Dawn analyzes the air samples in a machine that determines how much energy it takes for Primo to perform bouts of whistles. This session lasts for half an hour. When Primo's done, he swims to Beau for several mouthfuls of fish and back rubs. Other sessions throughout the week are done the same way, except, by way of comparison, Beau gives a different hand signal to both Primo and Puka, who then make louder sounds.

Back in Seattle, it's time to review the data. Marla looks at the visual recordings of the sounds to determine how loud and how long the whistles are. She also looks at how many whistles are produced. The study is twofold. While Marla looks at whistles, Dawn analyzes oxygen consumption data to determine how much energy it takes for each whistle bout.

Results show that Primo and Puka require more energy to make louder calls. Picture yourself making loud singing noises under this dome. If you sing really loudly for a few seconds, your body may find itself breathing more heavily. This is because your body requires more oxygen to fuel the increased energy used to sing louder. It could even make you tired. Dawn and Marla can infer that the same holds true for the whales. If we think about the heavy vessel traffic day when whale calls increase, we can say that the whales have to use more energy when vessels are around them. Dawn estimates that depending on its size and sex, a Southern Resident whale can eat eleven to sixteen Chinook salmon per day. She also believes that an increase in energy spent may mean that the Southern Residents need to eat extra fish. The problem is, there aren't always extra fish available.

In an effort to protect the Southern Residents, Dawn and Marla will continue to visit Primo and Puka for more answers as questions unfold. "Much of what we know about diving physiology, hearing, and sound production is the result of using trained animals in captivity. Without these studies, we would know far less about marine mammals than we do now," Dawn says. Marla believes that "the dolphins in Terrie's lab, a research lab, are important ambassadors for their free-ranging counterparts in the ocean. By involving them in research, you can dispel a variety of myths about marine mammals under human care, for they *are* much more than just a form of entertainment."

The Northern Resident whale Corky is held captive, and was once used for entertainment purposes, at Sea World in California. She is one of two resident whales currently in captivity. A release date for Corky has not been set.

LOLITA

Orcas were netted, then transported to marine parks for entertainment purposes.

Nearly fifty years ago, Lolita was seized in a net and subsequently sold. Lolita's situation is the result of the 1970 whale captures in Penn Cove, Washington. Throughout the course of ten years, 262 whales fell victim to these types of captures. Aquariums mostly in Canada and the United States bought fifty-three of the whales, and Lolita was one of the unlucky ones. Captors chose her because of her young age and docile nature, an asset that proved profitable for entertainment.

Bystanders in Washington State witnessed the brutal captures and became outraged, and soon government officials started to take action. In 1976, captures were banned, but the whale population had taken a huge hit owing to several deaths and injuries that ensued during the netting. Scientists believe that because of the captures, which entangled many of the J, K, and L pod members, the Southern Resident population has never fully recovered.

Howard Garrett and Susan Berta, founders of the Orca Network, are fighting to set Lolita free. She currently resides in an inhumanely small concrete tank in

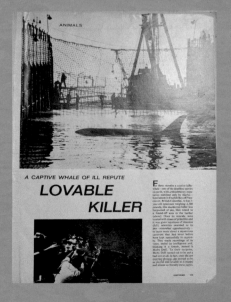

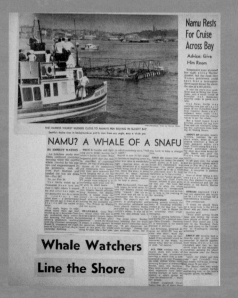

Headlines for the first captive orca whales. People were both fascinated and outraged.

Miami. She's more than three thousand miles (4,828 kilometers) away from her family. With the help of release experts, a plan is in place to bring her back to the wild where her L pod family lives. Experts believe that her family will find her and call to her. Currently, the Miami Seaquarium refuses to let her go. Howard and Susan continue their fight to set Lolita free. As Howard sees it, "As long as she hangs in there, we'll hang in there, and we're not giving up."

The plan goes as follows: First, the Miami Seaquarium staff will prepare Lolita in advance to teach her how to get positioned in a stretcher. Next, she'll be examined by a team of veterinarians to ensure that she's clear of all signs of pathogens. When her health report is given a score of 100 percent, she'll be led to her stretcher and lifted by a crane into a cradle of iced water on a truck trailer.

Then she'll be transported to Miami-Dade's International Airport, where she'll be loaded into a cargo aircraft and begin her flight to Bellingham International Airport, Washington. Trainers will remain at her side, keeping her calm. While being kept cool with ice, she'll travel for six hours. Upon arrival in Washington, her home state, she'll be transported from the aircraft to a truck trailer and driven to a barge, to be towed to the sea pen at Eastsound, Orcas Island. Here the crane will lift her seven-thousand-pound (3,175-kilogram) body in a sling and gently lower her into the sea pen of seawater from the waters where she was born. While in the sea pen she'll be cared for and monitored by a veterinarian. When she's hungry, she'll be fed live fish so that she can relearn the foraging techniques she'll need while with her family. She'll be given her usual dead frozen fish as a supplement until she no longer wants them.

As Lolita shows signs of good health and progress, trainers will begin boat-recall training within the netted area of the cove. This will teach her to come to the sea pen when an acoustic signal is made. When she's released into the open water, this signal will be sounded, and she'll know to return. Upon her return, she'll be examined for signs of stress. If Lol-

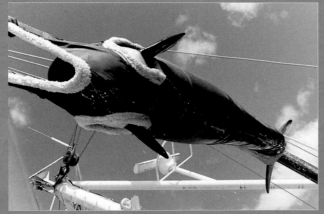

Sling being used to transport a whale.

ita appears fine, as anticipated, she'll be given the choice to leave if she desires. If she chooses at any point to stay, permanent care and companionship will be available. Experts believe that once Lolita's family hears her call, they'll come to find her and take her back home.

Lolita's home at the Miami Seaquarium

Scat detection dog Tucker.

Chapter 4

IT MAKES PERFECT SCENTS

On this crisp September morning, thirty minutes from San Juan Island's Snug Harbor, scratchy reception comes in from a VHF marine radio. The biologists Elizabeth Seely and Dr. Deborah Giles, otherwise known as "Giles," are led to believe that there are orcas swimming in the waters off Hein Bank. The two scientists steer the boat closer to that location. Giles cuts the motor to a steady and calm speed and Elizabeth opens a crate and leashes up the team's detection dog, Tucker. Without hesitation, the eager canine jumps onto the bow, leans over the metal bars, and goes to work. Today the two biologists are seeking out whale scat with the help of their trusty canine's trained nose. Tucker can pick up the most minuscule trace of scent from a distance of up to one nautical mile

Giles and Elizabeth travel through Hein Bank in search of whale scat.

Sam Wasser began collecting baboon scat in Africa to determine what was in the animals' DNA.

Tucker leans over the bow, his body posture pointing to the scat.

(1.8 kilometers) on the water. He's able to detect a scent five times quicker and farther away than humans. Elizabeth sits next to Tucker on the bow and wraps the leash around her left hand. She watches over her tail-wagging coworker, hoping to catch a signal that he's onto something.

As gross as it may seem, there's a wealth of information in a scooped-up glob of scat. Nearly twenty years ago, while doing a study in Africa, Dr. Sam Wasser, a researcher at the University of Washington (UW), began looking for information inside baboon scat. He was hoping to find answers without having to dart the animals, and this noninvasive approach yielded the information he'd hoped to find. What he discovered was that these dropped treasures were filled with DNA. He also determined levels of stress hormones and nutrition in an animal. Animals such as baboons and whales are constantly on the move and difficult to approach, so it makes sense to gather data this way. In 2006, after the Southern Residents were listed as endangered, Sam began analyzing whale scat at the University's lab. The project's been leading to significant findings ever since.

Today, as Tucker's detection work ensues, Giles steers the UW vessel *Moja* while Elizabeth leans close to Tucker. "Go find it," she says to him. She watches and waits for cues indicating that the dog smells a sample. In seconds, Tucker's nostrils begin to twitch—left, left, right, and left again. With each sniff, his nose moves faster. Soon enough, his black ears perk up and he slopes his body forward toward what might be a scent. When Tucker slants over the bow, his lips begin to twitch and his body posture changes to a stiff point. Giles steers based on Elizabeth's cues. Tucker's pointed stance eventually directs the team to the sample. Elizabeth announces, "There's one *huuuuge* one. Go left!" In under a minute they're close enough to collect the brown stuff the size of a dollar. Giles moves *Moja* closer. She shifts into neutral and grabs for a pole that has an attached plastic cup for scooping the sample. She needs to act fast; if she doesn't, the scat will likely sink in less than twenty minutes. Carefully, she ladles the sample and lifts it on deck. *Success!*

Tucker's tail is wagging, and his body is shaking back and forth, a clear indication that he's found the riches that lead to "Tucker time." Elizabeth grabs for his favorite toy, a green rubber ball with a string on the end. She puts it in his mouth and tugs back and forth. When she surrenders, Tucker shakes his head, whipping the string through the air. "That's a good boy, buddy! *Grrrrr,*" she says in a playful tone. When it comes to rewards for Tucker, "It's really all about the ball," she explains. This special toy is given to him as a reward only while on the boat. When Tucker gets the ball, he's enthusiastic. The magic ingredients that make him and other dogs in the program extra special is that they're hard-working and they're great sniffers. Most important, they'll work to play ball.

After playtime, Tucker relaxes in his crate. Off to the side, Elizabeth pours the salt water and scat into a funnel to eliminate most of the water. What remains goes into a fifty-

Giles steers *Moja* to the scat.

Scat, ladled out of the water, is used to gather information on the whales in a noninvasive way.

Tucker time! Scat detection dogs such as Tucker are intensely focused and have an insatiable urge to play. Their obsessive, high-energy temperaments make them difficult to maintain as family pets, and as a result, such dogs often end up at shelters.

Tucker relaxes after work and play.

milliliter plastic tube that is about three tablespoons full. It's then secured with a twist cap. This portion is added to a centrifuge, a tool that spins the sample and takes the liquid out, bringing it to a more solid state. In five minutes, the centrifuge stops. Giles takes out the tube, which is now free of water and salt, and adds it to the cooler. It's important to get all the water and salt out so that the sample is clean and easy to freeze. On average, Tucker finds at least two to three samples a day. This adds up to more than six hundred samples collected to date.

The crew's gone a whole day without getting close to a single whale, and that's okay. After working close to six hours, it's time for all of them to call it quits. At twelve years old, Tucker's still filled with plenty of energy, yet he's getting close to retirement age. Next season, a Blue Heeler male named Dio will be ready to step in and take over where Tucker leaves off.

Dio's been training to sniff out Southern Resident scat for the past seven months. To begin the training process, Elizabeth places scat in a floatable bowl upwind of the dog and the boat. When the bowl drifts, the scent travels downwind for the dog to smell. As the scat releases its scent, Giles steers away from the bowl to reposition the boat farther downwind by roughly two hundred yards (182 meters), about a football field and a half. They do this exercise until the dog is able to convey that he's detected the scent from five hundred yards (457 meters). As soon as the dog locates the smell of scat, Elizabeth and Giles watch his behaviors change. "It's a complicated dance—where we find scat in the end," Elizabeth says. For now, between training new dogs and collecting samples, they'll try to round up as much scat as possible. Next year, they're planning to travel farther into the waters bordering the United States and Canada to gather more samples.

After a full day, Tucker will sleep well tonight. "In my experience, working dogs don't make good pets," Elizabeth says. "Even when they're retired, they're a handful. They're in this program because the people who had them just couldn't handle them. Usually, when they aren't working anymore, their handlers adopt them and make it work." She laughs. "Even though they're crazy."

The crew heads back to Snug Harbor after covering the area around San Juan Island. Tucker sits on the boat in his crate for relaxation time. Elizabeth and Giles unpack their belongings and load up their cars. Elizabeth's the lucky winner who gets to take Tucker and the scat samples home. She'll store close to one hundred of them in her freezer. By

The detection dog Dio learns the tricks of the trade.

the season's end, when her freezer is jammed, she'll deliver the samples to the UW lab so others can uncover the mysteries of what's hidden inside.

A cold white fog escapes when the manager of the lab at UW's Center for Conservation Biology, Rebecca Booth, opens the lid of the -4°F (-20°C) freezer. Reaching in, she takes the scat samples out and places them in the centrifuge for another spin, removing any remaining water prior to freeze-drying. "It's this crazy process," Rebecca explains, "complete with a minus-fifty-eight-degree Fahrenheit [-50°C] coil and a vacuum pump that removes the air so the frozen water in the fecal sample gets sucked through the system as it freezes on the freezer coil." The freeze-drying lasts close to forty-eight hours, and the beauty is that it

Rebecca prepares samples for analysis at the University of Washington lab in Seattle.

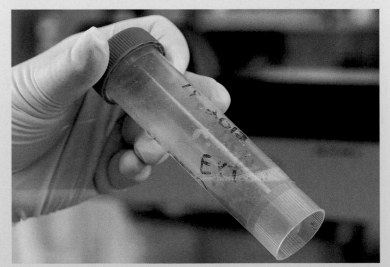

A typical whale scat sample is mostly water.

gets rid of the moisture. Freeze-drying, by eliminating excess water weight, provides more accurate estimates of the amount of hormone present. A small piece of the sample gets split up and sent to NOAA for DNA confirmation of the individual whale and sex of the animal.

For now, Rebecca is most concerned with hormone and stress level analysis. This process is based on precision, so she calculates water measurements at every stage. A typical whale scat sample is anywhere from 50 to 80 percent water. She removes the 80-milligram sample from the freeze dryer. "It's so small it's barely like a pencil eraser worth of sample," Rebecca says. This isn't a lot, considering that it's coming from a whale that can grow to be close to twelve thousand pounds (5,443 kilograms), about the size of a mobile home. Next, Rebecca adds a solution that will extract the hormones from the scat and indicate whether the sample is from a pregnant whale.

With every sample, the lab records and compares the health of the whales throughout the years. The UW lab has data going back to 2006, including when the whales are experiencing a time of "high food" or "low food." Each year, fish biologists continually collect data on the number of Chinook salmon present in various waterways. High food refers to a period of time when the Southern Resident food source of Chinook is plentiful; low food is a time when fish biologists report low counts of Chinook.

At the end of the analysis, Sam and Rebecca find that hormone levels indicate that many whales were pregnant throughout the spring Chinook salmon runs. Spring Chinook are the largest and fattiest stocks in the Fraser River. However, more than 60 percent of these pregnant Southern Residents will miscarry, which means that their calves will die before they're born. To Sam, "Nutritional stress from declining salmon runs seems to be the cause." This data shows Sam that there's a correlation between poor nutrition and high rates of miscarriages in the whales. It also tells him that when the Southern Residents are hungry, the whale population growth slows. With these findings, his study will hopefully help guide decisions that need to be made in order to promote the whales' recovery. First and foremost, he hopes these findings will raise awareness and enforce stricter regulations to promote salmon health, survival, and availability.

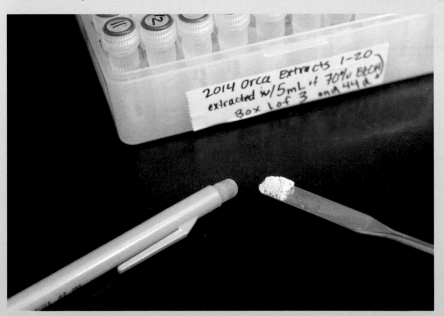

This small sample indicates hormone levels in a pregnant whale.

Chapter 5

MISSION MOBLEY SOARS

Picture yourself on a boat coasting away from the harbor. To your right, you see mountains, rocky beaches, pockets of trees, and sloping hillside meadows. You'll turn your head and look for signs of four-and-a-half-foot-(1.8-meter)-tall black razors slicing through the water's surface. There's nothing. The Southern Resident orca whales haven't been seen in days. Your gaze jumps to the trees, the mountains, then back to the water. After nearly half a day searching, there are still no Southern Residents. Finally, after three more hours, the boat captain and scientist Dr. Lance Barrett-Lennard spots four fins. They appear almost three boat lengths away. He, Dr. John Durban, and Dr. Holly Fernbach, both biologists, lift their binoculars. They recognize individuals based on Ken Balcomb's identification data. It's been well worth the wait.

Swimming at a speed of four knots (4.6 miles) per hour, in the lead, is one of the K family's oldest females, K-13 (Skagit). Her estimated birth year is 1972, which is one year prior to the beginning of the Center for Whale Research photo identification study. Skagit travels with her family group or matriline. With each breath, her family tree is revealed. There, beside his mom, is K-25 (Scoter), named after a popular bird; he is in his twenties. Farther out and to the left is his sister K-27 (Deadhead) and her son K-44 (Ripple). John and Holly watch and prepare

From one hundred feet above the whales, a hexacopter drone allows scientists to see Southern Resident K-13 (Skagit) and her family members swimming together. In this photo, Skagit's daughter Deadhead (K-27) swims next to K-44 (Ripple) in the top left. Close behind is Ripple's uncle Scoter (K-25) shown at the bottom right and his grandmother K-13 (Skagit) shown at the bottom left. Scoter travels more closely to his mother than any other member in the family. NOAA/Vancouver Aquarium, NMFS permit.

Lance, John, and Holly rely on a hexacopter drone to take photos without interfering in the whales' world.

for their next step. It's time to get Mobley ready for takeoff.

Who is Mobley? Mobley's a hexacopter drone powered by six quiet motors. It flies high over the whales and collects overhead photographs that can measure growth, fatness, and even pregnancy. At thirty-two inches (0.8 meters) across, Mobley is no bigger than a trash can lid and flies equipped with a high-resolution camera strapped to its underbelly. With calm seas and low wind, today is a perfect day to launch. Even though John and Holly don't go out in inclement weather, Mobley is built to withstand rain and high winds. John and Holly hope that Mobley can obtain an image of every individual in the Southern Resident population.

The primary objective of this research project is to determine whether members of the Southern Resident killer whale population are getting enough food to grow and reproduce successfully. To do this, the scientists keep a log consisting of measurements of each whale's body shape and how it changes across seasons and years. "Basically," John says, "what we're doing is using modern technology to answer the very simple question: What can we learn from the whale's shape?" Mobley's photos make it easy to identify individuals based on scratches, scars, and saddle patch variations. It's a method known as photogrammetry. In particular, John and Holly can positively document pregnant females by identifying whales that have their maximum girth behind their rib cage. Like humans, when female whales get pregnant, they carry their baby weight below their ribs. This

Mobley launches.

can be seen easily with overhead photography.

Several populations of Chinook salmon in Puget Sound have experienced critically low returns within the last twenty years. Many of the rivers where the Chinook populations live have had fewer than two hundred adult fish returning. Some scientists believe this is the result of dams blocking their travel patterns, as well as overfishing. Others say it's a result of fish farms planted in the ocean, causing disease among the wild populations. It's likely a combination of several factors. Overall, this decline is putting these fish populations at high risk. Until solutions are found, scientists such as John, Holly, and Lance continue to monitor how all this affects the Southern Residents.

While John straps the radio control around his neck, Holly begins a series of preflight checks. First she verifies the radio control link and battery level. Next, she sets up the video screen that shows her exactly what Mobley's camera sees. Once everything checks out okay and all visual systems are good to go, Holly picks up the drone and cups it in her hands. She raises her arms and prepares for liftoff. *Ready, set, TAKE FLIGHT.* John stands nearby, maneuvering the controls with his hand. He steers Mobley into the air and away from the boat. Within seconds, the aircraft soars above the whales. Holly takes a seat and views real-time data and video sent back to her monitor on the boat. She covers herself with a towel to shield the monitor from glare. To her right is Captain Lance; he's out to collect data on the Canadian-born Northern Residents that are not endangered. Recent findings suggest that the Northern Residents get a more adequate supply of food than the Southern Residents because of where they reside. John and Holly will compare their measurements with data from this other resident orca population.

As Mobley hovers one hundred feet (30 meters) above the whales, it snaps photos while under John's control. John stands behind Lance while he and Holly stay on target with the whales. Holly conveys directions to John: "Left . . . left . . . forward . . . now left; they're still in the middle of the frame." Deadhead branches off slightly, while five-year-old Ripple stays behind with his babysitters, Grandma Skagit and Uncle Scoter. This is proof that it takes an entire family to raise a Southern Resident calf. The whales put family first, and they do it with thought and skill. In John's opin-

Holly watches the screen under the blanket while Lance captains the boat and John flies the drone.

ion, "Southern Residents do family better than we do. They don't have to be that close. They can communicate over long distances, perhaps thousands of yards away from one another. They do this because they want to, and it's part of how they maintain social bonds."

The whales swim north. They're so close, they could reach out and touch one another. Next to the young Ripple, Scoter's body is massive, his pectoral fins the shape of giant Ping-Pong paddles, at five feet long and three feet wide (0.9 by 1.5 meters). He flanks the juvenile between himself and its grandmother. Ripple is no stranger to attention from his relatives. With the boat staying two hundred to three hundred yards (0.27 kilometers) away from the whales, John keeps Mobley flying above the K pod, within his sight at all times. "This is a view you can't get from a boat," he says. "When you look at the overhead images, it seems that anyone can become a scientist, easily seeing differences in whale size and shape. I don't think science needs to be complicated to be powerful." Best of all, the whales don't notice the drone. Holly continues to watch the live video feed on the monitor. While Mobley flies, the camera remains stable. In fifteen quick minutes, it's time for the drone to return and recharge. Holly comes out from under her fish-patterned blanket, and John flies Mobley back safely into Holly's hands.

With permission from NOAA and the Federal Aviation Administration (FAA), John flies Mobley with the understanding that he will keep the drone no less than one hundred feet (30 meters) above the whales. These permits are essential when working in close proximity to an endangered species such as the Southern Resident whales. Observing these wild marine mammals isn't always easy. When John and Holly started this project in collaboration with the Center for Whale Research, they photographed the whales from a helicopter. In order to avoid disturbing the whales, the helicopter flew at least 750 feet (229 meters) above them. This method was successful, and the images were fine, but there was one drawback: helicopters are expensive. In a quest to find a simple, cost-effective way to conduct their research, the scientists relied on the expertise of an engineer to create Mobley.

After three weeks of flying, the Mobley project is over for the season. John and Holly head back to their office at NOAA's Southwest Fisheries Science Center in La Jolla,

A photogrammetry image of the I-16 matriline of the Northern Resident pod. The Northern Resident pods aren't endangered like the Southern Residents. Northern Resident whales as seen in this image frequently travel in large pods of closely related individuals.
NOAA/Vancouver Aquarium, DFO permit.

California, where they discuss their findings. Although John leads a team of scientists on whale photogrammetry studies, he believes that the hardest part is now left to Holly's expertise. While looking over the crisp high-definition photographs, Holly measures tens of thousands of images in order to keep track of the whales' condition. She also catalogs images that provide insight into the lives of these whales, taking note of whales chasing and capturing salmon, calves nursing from their moms, and family groups swimming peacefully together.

While examining data from 2015 alongside Holly, John points to a photo of L-91 (Muncher) as she swims with her new calf, L-122 (Magic). John can tell that this photo was taken within a few days of the calf's birth because he's gray, mottled, and tiny. It's the smallest calf the team has ever measured, at seven feet long (2.1 meters). What John loves about this photo is the nurturing that can be seen as the calf swims up close to his mother's head. "This is just another indication of how Southern Resident moms are the calves' ticket to making it in the world," he says.

Other photos reveal two members of the family group bringing a partially eaten salmon to the new mom. They actually swim over and drop the salmon next to Muncher, and she picks it up. It's a great example of how the whole family is involved in raising this calf. It's believed that in the early days of calf rearing, a mother's time nursing her calf depletes her energy reserves, and their survival is dependent on the family's help.

Food sharing is a learned behavior among Southern Resident whales. This image shows new mother L-91 (Muncher) eating a salmon as her newborn calf L-122 (Magic) looks on. This fish was caught and given by other members of the family group. It shows how relatives help new moms by giving her fish so she doesn't need to stray from her calf. This image is used as a health assessment for the mother and calf. NOAA/Vancouver Aquarium, NMFS permit.

At NOAA's Southwest Fisheries Science Center, CA, John and Holly look at photometry data collected and compare whale measurements over time.

Next, John and Holly use the altitude measurements from Mobley to estimate the true lengths of the whales and monitor the growth of individuals over time. From their initial research with the helicopter, Holly has been able to construct a curve of average length for the known ages of the whales. The drone measurements are compared with the averages to see if the whales are growing as expected. Initially, whale length is measured using the photograph's pixels. The known altitude and focal length of the camera's lens are used to calculate a scale to convert pixels to real length.

When comparing measurements of shape, the whale's body condition can be assessed for short-term and long-term growth. This tells the scientists whether the whales are getting enough to eat. With less Chinook salmon in the waters over the years, whales are getting smaller. "There's this disturbing trend that more recently they're smaller in body size than they used to be," John says. This may be due to a lack of nutrition during the early growth period. As with humans, if there's insufficient food in early years, the individuals are likely to grow to a smaller adult size. When salmon stocks were more plentiful, it appeared that whales were growing bigger in their overall size and shape.

Judging by the photographs so far this fall, some whales look robust. However, John says that Polaris and her calf Dipper are worryingly thin. Sadly, both whales passed away that summer. John, Holly, Lance, and Mobley will head back into the field again next spring when the whales return from their winter-feeding areas. Ideally, the scientists will see consistent data showing whale growth and successful reproduction, correlating with healthy runs of Chinook salmon.

Perhaps in time, biologists will determine the best ways to recover the salmon population for the sake of people and whales. It is hoped that with this, an action plan will enable these whales to get an adequate food supply in their leanest times. Scientists will continue to examine the Southern Resident whale population's health for answers. Others will turn to Chinook salmon for answers.

Scientists will use photogrammetry images like this to take note of the growth of calf L-121 (Windsong) and the condition of her mother, L-94 (Calypso), while she nurses. On average, orca calves nurse for about two years before weaning off the milk. NOAA/Vancouver Aquarium, NMFS permit.

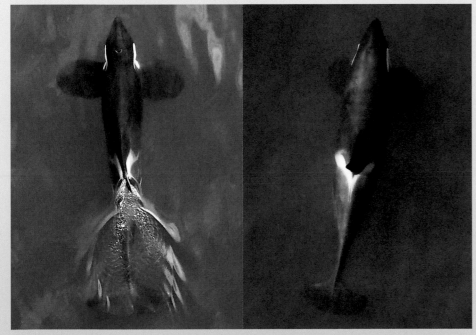

Two adult male orcas from the Northern Resident population show what scientists refer to as "contrasting body" condition. The whale on the left is in very poor condition as seen by its "peanut head" or depression in the skull. In contrast, the adult male on the right is very robust and appears to be well fed and healthy. NOAA/Vancouver Aquarium, DFO permit.

This photogrammetry image of Southern Resident orca L-41 (Mega) allows scientists to measure his dorsal (top) fin, curved flukes (back), and pectoral (side) fins. Each year, a health assessment is made based on the measurements made. NOAA/Vancouver Aquarium, NMFS permit.

From an ecotoxicologist's standpoint, Jessica Lundin says, "clean water is what the headlines should be about these days." Unfortunately, our oceans need some help in this department. In the world of fish studies, habitat restoration is one area being looked at and addressed. This is the process of rebuilding areas needed for fish to rest and feed in order to foster good health and growth. In other studies, scientists are examining the illnesses present in ocean-dwelling fish pens to see how the diseases spread to wild fish.

Jessica compares data with Gina, Sam, and Rebecca and is familiar with overall salmon and whale health. While Gina focuses on the chemical compound side and Sam and Re-

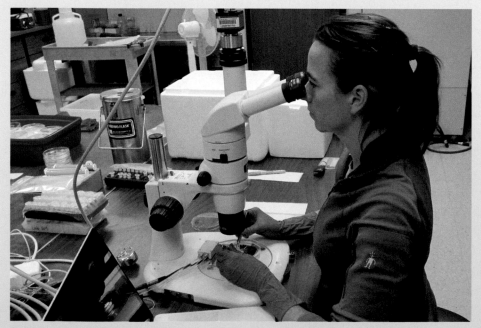

Jessica prepares samples to analyze contaminants present.

becca on the biological side, Jessica turns her attention to fish toxicants—the toxic substances such as DDT and PCBs introduced into the environment that affect fish on a large scale. By identifying ways to get these chemicals out of our waters, Jessica and others can ultimately save fish populations like Chinook salmon as well as the marine environment as a whole. In collaboration with other scientists, she believes that one of the biggest take-home messages is that we need more fish. Right now, her main focus is this: "If we took that toxicant away, how many more fish would survive and return to spawn eggs for the next generation?"

Projections are showing that a substantial number of fish could be saved if toxicants are taken out of the waters. To Jessica, the study of the toxicants in fish has an even broader impact because it's helping to save the whales and other animals, including people, all of whom depend on salmon. Come spring, she hopes to test various waterways in Oregon and Washington to see what toxicants she finds in individual fish. With that, she'll look to discover how these toxicants affect the health concerns of the entire population.

As Jessica continues to work on the science that might help influence policy and management decisions, she remains hopeful that restoration and remediation efforts will continue to clean up toxicants in our waters. The good news is, environmental groups have already begun restoring Alder Creek in Portland, Oregon, and have turned it into a salmon habitat. Continued cleanup of contaminants—as well as habitat restoration of salmon, bald eagles, and other animals harmed by contamination over time—is under way. The goal is to restore the creek to what it was prior to the contamination. Other efforts in the way of dam removals are also in progress. These are steps in the right direction. "We generate a lot of hypotheses," Jessica says, "and as we move forward, we will design new studies that will help important data gaps." It's a big step in the right direction, and with the science she provides, there's hope that less contaminated waters will follow.

The Alder Creek project is located in Portland, Oregon. The site was formerly occupied by a lumber mill. In 2012, after restoration, the site allows for salmon to have a place to feed and grow safely before heading into the ocean to be preyed upon.

THE LIFE OF A KING

It's spring in the Pacific Northwest, and the coastal waters are flooded with Chinook salmon. Heavy winds and cooler temperatures bring swift currents that tell many thousands of fish that it's time to embark on the journey of their lifetime. Few will make it back to the Columbia-Snake River Basin, the place they first called home. King salmon, one of the largest and fattiest salmon, will certainly try to return. His weight is half of that of his ancestors hundreds of years ago. He's only thirty pounds, today's average for a male his age. King is strong and resilient. For his lifetime of six years, he's beaten the odds of succumbing to the likes of hungry fishermen, watchful hawks, and ravenous Southern Resident whales.

King lives in the open ocean, fattening up on bait fish that will sustain the energy he needs to travel hundreds of miles a day. He's racing to make it to the freshwater spawning gravels, where he'll reproduce. He relies on his strong sense of smell to lead the way. His brain sends messages that release hormones into his body, and these hormones allow him to adjust to unsalted river surroundings. Even with his internal GPS, navigating in the open ocean is a difficult task for King as he sets out to identify the one stream he needs to enter. He has several thousand options to eliminate along the way and must not lose focus. He concentrates on the strength of the earth's magnetic field to guide him and take him back to where he was born.

Along the way, King swims uphill in a school of like-minded species; there is safety in numbers. The blue-gray and black-spotted bodies shimmy through

Chinook head upriver to spawn following the removal of the Elwha Dam in 2012.

Juvenile Chinook salmon

obstacles and jump through waterfalls. Several of King's schoolmates won't survive. Some veer off on different paths, cut short by roadblocks caused by years of dam destruction. Some will try to climb up ladders created to help them break through these barriers. If the velocity of the water falling over the steps is too great, they will grow exhausted. Weary and unable to continue upriver, they perish in the rushing waters.

King swims near the rocky edge, close to a hawk with a four-foot wingspan that is circling above the water. Like a knight with swords armed for battle, the hawk curls his talons, tucks his wings, and dive-bombs toward the water in an effort to anchor the King. By a narrow margin, King misses the hawk's capture and swirls until he crashes into a bed of rocks. This force blows him off course. He checks his magnetic position to stay on track with the migration. In seconds, instinct kicks in and he gathers his strength. This is no time to quit. The bruised and battled soldier moves onward with the rest of the troops. Finally, after swimming nearly a thousand miles upriver and climbing more than six thousand feet in elevation, King reaches a shallow bed of gravel. He can finally rest in the place where he was born years ago.

He's starving but refuses to eat. Eating would also require time to hunt, and time is against him. He's almost made it to the finish line and must find a mate. By now his fleshy pink pigment moves to his skin and dresses him in a fire-engine-red suit. He's a handsome king. Like a bird with bright plumes, his radiant hues make him showy enough to attract the attention of a nearby female who is shoveling a nest with her tail. He guards her as she digs tirelessly, until her tail wears down to a stump. King watches and prepares to battle other males who may try to encroach on his spawning opportunity. When King's mate deposits her five thousand eggs, King swims over to fertilize. Mission complete. He and his mate are getting closer to the end of their lives.

As the days grow shorter, King's skin and meat shed from his body and settle into the sediment. These nutrients will feed his offspring, which will hatch in four months and grow into tiny fry. After three days, King dies. His body remains in a mound. Fish like King are a gift to our precious and fragile ecosystem.

Chapter 6

WHAT THE FUTURE HOLDS

By late September, field research is tapering down for the season. For the Southern Resident orca pods, winter will bring cooler water temperatures and rougher seas. As they disperse into smaller pod groups from their summer residence in the San Juan Islands, they'll continue to hunt, socialize, forage, and play. In February, Brad and other NOAA scientists will go out on a winter cruise in an effort to find the whales. It's not known for certain where the orcas go during the winter, and Brad hopes to get closer to finding answers. Tagging devices offer insight into the whales' whereabouts. Many believe this invasive practice carries too much risk. In time, Brad hopes to perfect the tags and eventually track the whales in the most efficient way. Until then, tagging is put on hold. For now and in years to come, all the data collected on every Southern Resident is held in a database at the University of California, Davis. In this system each Southern Resident whale has its own health record and will be monitored from year to year. With each passing year, evidence becomes clearer that this orca population lacks an adequate supply of food. Studies also suggest that the whales use more energy when in the presence of vessels and that they show high levels of toxicants in their bodies. Future studies will also try to determine whether vessel fuel in the water has an impact on pregnant whales and their calves.

Saving the whales is not an impossible feat, yet it's a process that takes time. As Dawn says, "Most of us, especially in this field, do what we do because we are passionate about the environment and are trying to improve the planet and help animals." With this, we can hold on to the notion that there will be changes made for the better,

Dawn says, "Most of us, especially in this field, do what we do because we are passionate about the environment and are trying to improve the planet and help animals."

and hopefully soon. While the fate of the fish and whales remains uncertain, we know that in the past, several animal species—including various fish, the humpback whale, and the bald eagle—have successfully come off the endangered species list as a result of hard work, increased awareness, and persistence. In the end, it depends on the efforts of the scientists, government officials, and concerned citizens coming together to make a difference.

Ken believes that prey resources are the most critical factor in the whales' survival over the past few years, and that the lack of a food supply needs to be addressed sooner than later. "It totally relates to the fish," he says. Ken and Giles are working to bring awareness to this situation. Giles believes that "the biggest problem is that the fish are dwindling, and we're barely modifying our fisheries quotas." As a result, the wild salmon population is "being watered down." This is due to mixed breeding—with the genetically altered population mixing into the ocean waters and carrying diseases that are killing off the wild population. Giles believes that stronger fisheries management practices are necessary to stop the hatchery fish from competing with the wild salmon. Many biologists are fighting for change and not being heard. Giles hopes that young people may hold the answer to getting things done: "Often, when kids start demanding answers and solutions, people pay better attention." She urges kids to use their voice to spread the word to make change happen.

In the meantime, biologists such as Ken and Giles believe

that officials need to start by organizing efforts to breach dams that run along Idaho and the eastern end of Washington State. They and others also think it's critical to start putting stricter limits on fishing in the Fraser River in British Columbia. There are a lot of layers to this problem, and Ken says he's willing to do what it takes to get the whales fed before it's too late. "If I have to go down and stand on the steps of the government mansion or go to [Washington] D.C. to stand outside the fence with a sign, I'm going to encourage our government officials to feed these whales and recover our ecosystem," he says. "We live in an ecosystem where everything depends on everything else being healthy and viable; we can't continue to consume the planet and contaminate it and expect that humans are going to survive."

The future of this population depends on the vigilance of many. It relies on people like us to spread the word, get involved in local cleanups, and tell others how magnificent these animals are. As scientists move forward in their discoveries, we can only hope to continue to learn from the intelligent and awe-inspiring Southern Resident whales. What the whales are showing us matters. We owe it to them, to ourselves, and to the planet to listen.

Clean and healthy oceans are essential to the survival of both whales and people.

HOW TO GET INVOLVED AND STAY INFORMED

There are many ways for you and your family to stay involved and keep informed about the Southern Resident orca whale community. First, there is the Center for Whale Research, which relies on donations not only to keep the center and the boats running but also to allow staff members such as Ken, Giles, and Dave Ellifrit to photograph, keep count, and be available for sightings twenty-four hours a day throughout the year. To learn more about this program and receive daily updates and photographs of whale encounters, visit the Center for Whale Research site at www.whaleresearch.com.

Another great organization that offers education on the Southern Resident community and related issues is the Orca Network. The network members are advocates for change when it comes to protecting and increasing awareness of the Southern Resident killer whales and their habitat. They're also still working to save Lolita, and they provide updates and offer ways for the community to get involved on various issues across the globe. The Orca Network site can be visited at www.orcanetwork.org.

If you'd like to consider adopting an orca, the Whale Museum (www.whalemuseum.org) offers a Southern Resident orca adoption program in which the museum works to inform and protect the Southern Resident community through outreach, education, and research.

To learn more about wild salmon and ways to save the salmon population, visit the Save Our Wild Salmon site at www.wildsalmon.org. Save Our Wild Salmon works with organizations throughout the nation to restore wild salmon to the rivers, streams, and oceans.

If you and your family like eating fish, keep eating it, but try to choose sustainably harvested salmon and other seafood to help protect wild fish populations. Visit www.seafoodwatch.org for up-to-date information on which fish are good to eat and which are best to avoid. By choosing what's referred to as a sustainable seafood, you can be sure that you're eating seafood that won't jeopardize the health and function of our oceans and whales.

If you or someone you know has unused medication, look for a household hazardous waste collection facility in your community that will take your old or unused chemicals. Dumping these hazardous chemicals into household toilets and sinks, or outside, where they can get into ditches or storm drains, is not advised and can pollute local waterways.

If you're lucky enough to see an orca someday, alert the researchers at the Center for Whale Research or the Orca Network so scientists can track its travel.

Get involved in efforts to protect and restore habitat in your community. Your help matters!

GLOSSARY

breach a whale exposes two-thirds of its body as it leaps out of the water.

calf a young whale, typically born in fall or winter.

carnivorous mammal-eating.

cetacean a whale, dolphin, or porpoise.

clan one or more pods that share a dialect.

community a group of pods that travel together.

DDT (dichlorodiphenyltrichloroethane) an insecticide banned in the United States in the 1970s. Owing to biopersistence, DDTs can still be found at high levels in the environment.

dialect a unique set of calls made by an individual whale and fellow pod members.

dorsal fin the fin on the back of the whale.

echolocation the process by which toothed animals such as killer whales make sounds to obtain information about their surroundings.

ecotoxicoloist a scientist who specializes in the study of the harmful effects of chemical, biological, and physical agents on living organisms, including humans.

fluke print the print left on the surface of the water after a tail slap.

flukes the horizontal projections that form a whale's tail.

forage to search for food.

hydrophone an underwater microphone used to listen to and record vocalizations.

juvenile an immature whale of either sex.

matriline a social unit of animals composed of a mature female and her immediate descendents.

necropsy the surgical dissection of a corpse to determine the cause of death.

offshore pod a pod seen in outer coastal waters.

PBDEs (polybrominated diphenyl ethers) flame retardants, used in everything from couches to baby clothes, but later found to have toxic effects and subsequently banned in the United States.

PCB a chemical used broadly in electrical apparatuses, paints, and numerous household items before being banned (most uses) in the United States in the 1970s. Because of biopersistence, PCBs can still be found at high levels in the environment.

photogrammetry the science of making measurements from photographs.

piscivorous fish-eating.

pod a social group of whales.

resident pod a group of killer whales that feed on fish, mainly salmon, and remain stable over time; found in both northern and southern regions.

toxicant a toxic substance introduced into the environment.

toxin a poisonous substance produced in living cells or organisms.

scat an animal fecal dropping used for scientific study.

sea pen an area that houses marine animals in their natural environment with the use of a net.

specimen a limited quantity of something used to represent a larger amount.

spectrogram a visual representation of the spectrum of frequencies in a sound or other signal as it varies with time.

subpod one or more matrilineal groups that temporarily separate from a pod.

transient pod a group of killer whales that feed mainly on marine mammals and travel in a constantly changing social structure.

SELECTED BIBLIOGRAPHY AND SOURCES

All personal interview quotations were taken from interviews conducted with scientists by the author at Friday Harbor during the week of June 11-17, 2016, or from follow-up telephone calls and email correspondence.

Barre, Lynn. "Southern Resident Killer Whale Recovery." *Endangered Species Bulletin,* Summer 2009: 26-27.

Center for Whale Research. "About Killer Whales/Orca." (www.whaleresearch.com; accessed March 2017)

Duncan, Sally L., D. H. Lach, and R. T. Lackey, eds. *Salmon 2100: The Future of Wild Pacific Salmon.* 1st edition. Bethesda, MD: American Fisheries Society, 2006.

Estes, James. *Whales, Whaling, and Ocean Ecosystems.* Berkeley: University of California Press, 2006.

Ford, John K. B., Graeme M. Ellis, and Ken C. Balcomb. *Killer Whales.* Vancouver, Canada: UBC Press, 1994.

Frizzelle, Christopher. "The Fight to Free Lolita." *Stranger,* September 30, 2015. (www.thestranger.com; accessed April 2016)

Garrett, Howard. *Residents and Transients–How Did That Happen?* Vol. 3 of *Orcas in Our Midst.* Orca Network, 2011: 1-33.

Gorman, Brian. "NOAA Fisheries Service Seeks Comment on Chinook Salmon Bycatch Management Plan." NOAA Fisheries Service, March 23, 2010. (www.nmfs.noaa.gov; accessed October 2016)

Holt, Marla, and Dawn Noren. "Speaking Up: Killer Whales (*Orcinus orca*) Increase Their Call Amplitude in Response to Vessel Noise." *Journal of American Statistical Association.* (www.swfsc.noaa.gov; accessed December 2008)

Hoyt, Erich. *Orca: The Whale Called Killer.* Ontario, Canada: Camden House Publishing, 1990: 20.

Lewis, Paul Owen. *Storm Boy.* Berkeley, CA: Tricycle Press, 1995.

Lundin, Jessica I., Gina M. Ylitalo, Rebecca K. Booth, Bernadita Anulacion, Jennifer A. Hempelmann, Kim M. Parsons, Deborah A. Giles, Elizabeth A. Seely,

M. Bradley Hanson, Candice K. Emmons, and Samuel K. Wasser. "Modulation in Persistent Organic Pollutant Concentration and Profile by Prey Availability and Reproductive Status in Southern Resident Killer Whale Scat Samples." *Environmental Science & Technology* 50 (12) (2016): 6506-16. (pubs.acs.org/doi/abs/10.1021/acs.est.6b00825; accessed September 2017).

Neiwert, David A. *Of Orcas and Men: What Killer Whales Can Teach Us.* New York: Overlook, 2015.

NOAA. "Elwha River Restoration." Northwest Fisheries Science Center. (www.nwfsc.noaa.gov; accessed April 2015)

NOAA. "Recovery Plan for Southern Resident Killer Whales (*Orcinus orca*)." National Marine Fisheries Service Northwest Regional Office. 2008. (www.nmfs.noaa.gov; accessed 2017)

Norren, Dawn, A. H. Johnson, D. Rehder, and A. Larson. "Close Approaches by Vessels Elicit Surface Active Behaviors by Southern Resident Killer Whales." *Endangered Species Research* 8 (2009): 179-92.

One Ocean. "Whale Songs." March 19, 2010. (YouTube; accessed March 29, 2016)

Orca Network. "John Durban at Ways of Whales 2015 Part I." January 24, 2015. (YouTube, www.orcanetwork.org; accessed July 15, 2016)

Orca Network. "Lolita's Transport and Retirement—Step by Step." (n.d.) n. pag. Print.

Portland Harbor Natural Resources. "Alder Creek Restoration Project." Portland Harbor Natural Resource Trustee Council, July 2014. (www.fws.gov; accessed October 24, 2016)

Press, Rich. "Transcript: UAV Reveals Killer Whales in Striking Detail." NOAA Fisheries. (Podcast, nmfs.noaa.gov; accessed October 26, 2016)

Save Our Wild Salmon. "The Orca Connection." (www.wildsalmon.org; accessed April 20, 2017)

Stiffler, Lisa. "PBDEs: They Are Everywhere, They Accumulate and They Spread." *Seattle Post-Intelligencer*, March 27, 2007. (www.seattlepi.com; accessed October 25, 2016)

The Whale Museum. "Meet the Whales." (www.whalemuseum.org, accessed July 2, 2015)

ACKNOWLEDGMENTS & AUTHOR'S NOTE

When I started writing this book, I didn't intend for it to end with an unanswered set of questions, the answers to which will determine the fate of these awesome creatures and their habitat. I also didn't expect for any of the whales in the book, namely Polaris, her calf Dipper, Granny, and Sonic, to no longer be alive. Their deaths are an example of how, in a short time, so much in our environment can change. My gratitude goes out to all the scientists who are the first to tell us that it's not too late to make a difference.

First and foremost, Andy and I would like to thank Ken Balcomb for allowing us to observe and ask questions, sharing his time, and offering the Center's photographs. Ken, this book wouldn't exist without you. Also, many thanks go out to the entire staff at the Center for Whale Research, especially Deborah Giles and Dave Ellifrit. A big thanks to the folks at NOAA, including Lynne Barre, Brad Hanson, Candi Emmons, Dawn Noren, Marla Holt, and Gina Ylitalo for insight into your studies. Thanks for the photos and information from John Durban, Holly Fernbach, and Lance Barrett-Lennard. To Sam Wasser, Rebecca Booth, Elizabeth Seely, and Jessica Lundin who invited us into the field and laboratory. Thanks to the Whale Museum and the Orca Network and to the inspirational Rosie Cayou from the Samish Indian Nation for allowing me to write about the Samish naming ceremony. Natalie VanderLey, thanks for offering your insight. To my alma mater, the University of Washington, for offering endless opportunities that have helped me succeed, starting with David Baine. I can't go without giving five stars to Erica Zappy Wainer for believing in this project and making it work. To the photographer Andy Comins, thank you; your time and talent are much appreciated. To my writing friends, Diane Telgan, Todd Garring, Katina Presutti, Jocelyn Rish, and Loree Griffin Burns. For understanding and guidance from Diane and Joe Dillon, Suzy Fairbanks, Emily Hatton, and the Star Girls. To Jim and my family for believing in me and always coming along for the ride. To my dear Poppi, the late Michael Perez, thanks for giving me the inspiration and foundation to kindle my creative spirit that allowed me to nurture my love for writing. Of course, I cannot end without thanking my boys: Nick, Evans, Christopher. Jimmy—thanks for being magnificent.

Last but not least, to all to the readers of this book: you are the ones who care, the ones who listen and thrive on learning. You are the ones who will make a difference in the future of our world, and for that, thank you.

PHOTO CREDITS

All images by Andy Comins except for the following:

Page 1: Barbara Todd, Center for Whale Research, Photo taken under Federal Permits/NMFS Permit 15569; page 2: Dave Ellifrit, Center for Whale Research, Photo taken under Federal Permits/NMFS Permit 15569; page 4: Graeme Ellis: page 5: Diane Claridge, Center for Whale Research; page 10 (top): Dave Ellifrit, Center for Whale Research, Photo taken under Federal Permits/NMFS Permit 15569; page 11 (bottom): Ken Balcomb, Center for Whale Research; page 13 (right): Center for Whale Research, Photo taken under Federal Permits NMFS Permit 15569; page 14: Dave Ellifrit, Center for Whale Research, Photo taken under Federal Permits NMFS/Permit 15569; pages 16, 17 (top): Dave Ellifrit, Center for Whale Research, Photos taken under Federal Permits NMFS/Permit 15569; page 17 (bottom): Ken Balcomb, Center for Whale Research, Photo taken under Federal Permits/NMFS Permit 15569; page 20 (top left, top right, bottom right): Ken Balcomb, Center for Whale Research, Photos taken under Federal Permits/NMFS Permit 15569; page 20 (bottom left): Dave Ellifrit, Center for Whale Research, Photo taken under Federal Permits/NMFS Permit 15569; page 21: Chris McCool; page 24: Dave Ellifrit, Center for Whale Research, Photo taken under Federal Permits NMFS Permit 15569; page 25 (right): Paula Crozier; page 26 (bottom): Robert Hunt, NOAA Fisheries NWFS, NWFS Permit 161; page 27 (bottom): Jeannie Hyde, courtesy of Center for Whale Research, Photo taken under Federal Permits/NMFS Permit 15569; page 28 (bottom): Dave Ellifrit, Center for Whale Research, Photo taken under Federal Permits NMFS/Permit 15569; page 34: Dave Ellifrit, Center for Whale Research, Photo taken under Federal Permits NMFS/Permit 15569; page 36 (top left): Ken Balcomb, Center for Whale Research, Photo taken under Federal Permits/NMFS Permit 15569; page 36: Dave Ellifrit, Center for Whale Research, Photos taken under Federal Permits NMFS/Permit 15569; page 37: Dave Ellifrit, Center for Whale Research, Photo taken under Federal Permits NMFS/Permit 15569; pages 39, 43: Dawn Noren, NOAA Fisheries; page 42: Ken Balcomb, Center for Whale Research, Photo taken under Federal Permits/NMFS Permit 15569; page 45: Wallie V. Funk Collection, Center for Pacific Northwest Studies, Western Libraries Heritage Resources; page 46: Lynne Barrie, NOAA Fisheries; page 47 (right): Maggie Evans; page 50 (top): Courtesy of Dr. Sam Wasser, University of Washington; page 53 (bottom) Elizabeth Seeley, The Center for Conservation Biology, Conservation Canines, University of Washington; page 58 (top): John Durban, NOAA/Vancouver Aquarium, NMFS Permits 16163, 19091; page 58 (bottom): Paul B. Hillman; pages 59, 60: Paul B. Hillman; page 61: John Durban, NOAA/Vancouver Aquarium, DFO Permit; page 62 (top): John Durban, NOAA/Vancouver Aquarium, NMFS Permits 16163, 19091; page 63 (left): John Durban, NOAA/Vancouver Aquarium, DFO Permit, (right) John Durban, NOAA/Vancouver Aquarium, NMFS Permits 16163, 19091; page 64: Sarah Fish; page 65 (top and bottom, right): Courtesy of Wildlands Inc; page 66: John McMillan/NOAA; page 71 (top): Jeannie Hyde; page 71 (bottom): Ken Balcomb, Center for Whale Research, Photo taken under Federal Permits/NMFS Permit 15569.

INDEX

Note: Page references in **bold** indicate photographs and their captions.

A

Alder Creek project, 64, **65**

B

Balcomb, Ken, 5-6, **8,** 9-16, **10, 13,** 70-71
Barrett-Lennard, Lance, 56, 59, **60**
Bigg, Mike, **4,** 4-6, 11
blubber biopsies, 25, 31-33
Booth, Rebecca, **54,** 54-55

C

Center for Whale Research (CWR), 9, **12, 28,** 72
Chinook salmon, 13, 55, 59, 62, 63, 64, **66,** 66-67
comb jellies, 25, **25**
communication and sounds, 14-15, 35-44
contaminants, 31-33, 64-65, 72
Corky, **44**

D

DDTs, 31-32
Dio the dog, 52-53, **53**
dolphins, 41-44, **43**
Durban, John, 56-63, **60, 62**

E

Eclipse, 22, **24**
Emmons, Candi, 22-28
endangered species, 16, 50

F

Fernbach, Holly, 56-63, **60, 62**
fish scales, 24-26, **26**
fluke print, 27, **27**
Fraser River, 13, 71

G

Giles, Deborah, **49,** 49-53, **51,** 70-71
Granny, 35-37, **37**

H

Hanson, Brad, 22-28, 31, **31,** 69
hexacopter drone, **58,** 58-62
Holt, Marla, 38-44, **39, 40**
hydrophone, 38, **39**

K

King salmon, 66-67

L

Lolita, 45-47, 72
Lundin, Jessica, 63-65, **64**

M

Miami Seaquarium, 46-47, **47**
Mobley, **58,** 58-62

N

National Oceanic Atmospheric Administration (NOAA), 9
necropsies, 11
Noren, Dawn, 35-44, **38, 41,** 69-70, **70**
Northern Residents, 5, 30, **61, 63**
Nova, 22, **24**
nutrition analysis, 50, 55

O

orcas, 5, 18, 19, 30. *See also* Northern Residents; Southern Residents

P

PBDEs, 32
PCBs, 31-32
photogrammetry, 58
photo identification, 4-5, 9-11, 56-63
pods, 5
Polaris, 10, **13,** 14, **14,** 62
Primo, 41-44, **43**
Princess Angeline, 14, 15, **16, 17**
Puka, 41-44

R

rake marks, 15, **20**
resident orcas, 5

S

S1 call, **40,** 40-41
S2iii call, 39, **40**
saddle patches, 19, **20**
Salish Sea, 5-6, 13
salmon, 13, 66-67, 72. *See also* Chinook
   salmon
Samish naming ceremony, 11, 21
scat, 27, 49-55, **51, 54**
Seely, Elizabeth, **49,** 49-54
Skagit, 56, **58**
Southern Residents, 5, 18
   communication among, 14-15, 35-44
   family orientation, 14, 60, 61
   fish sharing, 22, **24**
   food sources, 13, 30
   health assessments, 25
   infant mortality rate, 33, 55
   juvenile males, 15, **17**
   names given to, 10-11, 21
   photo identification, 9-11, 25-27, 56-63
   population decline, 16
   staying informed about, 72
   superpod encounters, **11,** 13-14
Star, 14, **14,** 15, **20**
stress hormones, 50, 55

superpods, **11,** 13-14
surface-active behaviors (SABs), 35-38,
   36

T

toxins, 31-33, 64-65, 72
transient orcas, 5, 30
Tucker the dog, 49-54, **50, 52, 54**

W

Wasser, Sam, 50, **50,** 55
Whale Museum, 10-11, 72
Williams, Terrie, 42

Y

Ylitalo, Gina, **31,** 31-33

SCIENTISTS IN THE FIELD

Where Science Meets Adventure

Check out these titles to meet more scientists who are out in the field—and contributing every day to our knowledge of the world around us:

Looking for even more adventure? Craving updates on the work of your favorite scientists, as well as in-depth video footage, audio, photography, and more? Then visit the Scientists in the Field website!

sciencemeetsadventure.com